Cambridge Elements 

Elements in Ethics
edited by
Ben Eggleston
University of Kansas
Dale E. Miller
Old Dominion University, Virginia

SIDGWICK'S ETHICS

Anthony Skelton
University of Western Ontario

CAMBRIDGE
UNIVERSITY PRESS

Shaftesbury Road, Cambridge CB2 8EA, United Kingdom

One Liberty Plaza, 20th Floor, New York, NY 10006, USA

477 Williamstown Road, Port Melbourne, VIC 3207, Australia

314–321, 3rd Floor, Plot 3, Splendor Forum, Jasola District Centre,
New Delhi – 110025, India

103 Penang Road, #05–06/07, Visioncrest Commercial, Singapore 238467

Cambridge University Press is part of Cambridge University Press & Assessment,
a department of the University of Cambridge.

We share the University's mission to contribute to society through the pursuit of
education, learning and research at the highest international levels of excellence.

www.cambridge.org
Information on this title: www.cambridge.org/9781009517706

DOI: 10.1017/9781108580588

When citing this work, please include a reference to the DOI 10.1017/9781108580588

First published 2025

A catalogue record for this publication is available from the British Library

ISBN 978-1-009-51770-6 Hardback
ISBN 978-1-108-70635-3 Paperback
ISSN 2516-4031 (online)
ISSN 2516-4023 (print)

Sidgwick's Ethics

Elements in Ethics

DOI: 10.1017/9781108580588
First published online: February 2025

Anthony Skelton
University of Western Ontario

Author for correspondence: Anthony Skelton, askelto4@uwo.ca

Abstract: Henry Sidgwick's *The Methods of Ethics* is one of the most important and influential works in the history of moral philosophy. *The Methods of Ethics* clarifies and tackles some of the most enduring and difficult problems of morality. It offers readers a high-calibre example of analytical moral philosophy. This Element interprets and critically evaluates select positions and arguments in Sidgwick's *The Methods of Ethics*. It focuses specifically on Sidgwick's moral epistemology, his argument against common-sense morality, his argument for utilitarianism, his argument for rational egoism, and his argument for what he calls "the dualism of practical reason," the thesis that utilitarianism and rational egoism are coordinate but conflicting requirements of rationality. *Sidgwick's Ethics* attempts to acquaint readers with the scholarly and theoretical debates relating to Sidgwick's theses while providing readers with a greater appreciation of the depth and sophistication of Sidgwick's masterpiece.

This Element also has a video abstract: www.cambridge.org/
EETH_Skelton_abstract

Keywords: Sidgwick, utilitarianism, egoism, common-sense morality, dualism of practical reason, intuitionism

ISBNs: 9781009517706 (HB), 9781108706353 (PB), 9781108580588 (OC)
ISSNs: 2516-4031 (online), 2516-4023 (print)

Contents

Introduction

This Element focuses primarily on Henry Sidgwick's (1838–1900) *The Methods of Ethics*, one of the most important and inspiring works in the history of moral philosophy.[1] Since Sidgwick is less well known than other historically important contributors to moral philosophy, such as Immanuel Kant and John Stuart Mill, this Element begins with some facts about his life. Once these are described, we will be able to state why *The Methods of Ethics* is, of the many works Sidgwick authored, worthy of our focus.

Henry Sidgwick was born on 31 May 1838 in Skipton, Yorkshire, where his father, William Sidgwick, was the headmaster of the Skipton grammar school. His extended family on his father's side had deep roots in Yorkshire where they ran mills spinning cotton yarn. After his father died in 1841, Sidgwick's mother, Mary Sidgwick (née Crofts), decided it best for the family to leave Yorkshire, eventually relocating them to Rugby in Warwickshire, where Sidgwick attended Rugby School. When he graduated from Rugby in 1855, Sidgwick entered Trinity College, Cambridge to study classics and mathematics.

Sidgwick had by all accounts an outstanding career as an undergraduate, winning many scholarships and prizes. His academic success was not, however, the only important feature of his time at Cambridge. While he was a student, Sidgwick joined the somewhat secret discussion society known as The Apostles, and the impact on him was lasting. The society's spirit, which, he said, "absorbed and dominated" him involved the

> pursuit of truth with absolute devotion and unreserve by a group of intimate friends, who were perfectly frank with each other, and indulged in any amount of humorous sarcasm and playful banter, and yet each respects the other, and when he discourses tries to learn from him and see what he sees. Absolute candour was the only duty that the tradition of the society enforced. (M 34)

Sidgwick's participation in the society was personally transformative, revealing to him that, as he put it, "the deepest bent of my nature was towards the life of thought – thought exercised on the central problems of human life" (M 35). To thinking and writing about both the theoretical and practical aspects of these problems Sidgwick devoted his academic career, all of which he spent as faculty at Trinity College, rising, in 1883, to Knightsbridge Professor of Moral Philosophy, a position he held until shortly before his death from cancer on 28 August 1900.

Sidgwick lectured and published on an enormous range of topics, including classics, economics, educational reform, philosophy, poetry, politics, and psychical

---

[1] References to Sidgwick's works appear as abbreviations, which are provided below in the References section of this *Element*.

phenomena. His major publications include *The Methods of Ethics* (1874), *The Principles of Political Economy* (1883), *Outlines of the History of Ethics* (1886), *The Elements of Politics* (1891), and *The Development of European Polity* (1903).

In addition to making contributions to scholarship, Sidgwick invested time and energy into advancing higher education for women and conducting parapsychological research (including the investigation of mediums and alleged instances of telepathy). Together with his wife, Eleanor (Nora) Mildred Sidgwick (née Balfour), whom he married in 1876, Sidgwick helped to found Newnham College at Cambridge and was instrumental in getting women permission to attend lectures and to write exams at Cambridge. However, he could not prevail in getting them admitted to degrees.

Sidgwick had a lifelong interest in paranormal phenomenon and parapsychological research. He was one of the founders of the Society for Psychical Research in 1882 and served as its first president. One of his main aims in conducting this research, again with Nora, was to see whether he might find empirical evidence for an existence after physical death and for God. This might, he thought, provide evidence for a coincidence between moral demands and self-interest, a matter that, as we shall see, deeply troubled him. Although he spent much time and effort on this research, he did not believe he found the evidence which he sought.

In 1859, when he graduated with firsts in classics and mathematics, Sidgwick was elected to a Fellowship at Trinity and at the same time he was made lecturer in classics. By 1865, his interest turned to philosophy and in 1867 he swapped his lectureship in classics for one in moral sciences (which included philosophy, politics, and economics). He never looked back. Sidgwick worked in many areas of philosophy (including the history of philosophy and epistemology), but his most lasting contributions are to moral philosophy. These contributions are found primarily in *The Methods of Ethics*. He revised the work five times during his life. The seventh edition appeared posthumously in 1907 and it is on this edition that scholars rely.

Sidgwick's *Methods* had its origin in a practical ethical problem that he faced. He described the decade between the time he was elected to his Trinity Fellowship and 1869 as a period of "storm and stress" (M 33). To take up a Fellowship one was required to subscribe to the Thirty-Nine Articles of the Church of England (including belief in the resurrection of Christ and the virgin birth). By 1869, after careful attempts in the early 1860s to determine the truth in Christianity, Sidgwick concluded he could no longer subscribe to all the Articles (especially not to belief in the virgin birth). This led to a vexing dilemma.

There are, Sidgwick thought, benefits of having intelligent people in Fellowship positions like the one he occupied, including individuals intelligent enough to entertain doubt about the Articles. But to subscribe to the Articles to take up or retain a Fellowship despite one's doubts seems dishonest. Is it permissible, he wondered, for intelligent people with doubts to accept or retain Fellowships if doing so involved the cost of dishonestly subscribing to the Articles? Sidgwick did not believe he could resolve this dilemma by appeal to common-sense morality. He had to look elsewhere. Ultimately, he decided that the harm of dishonest subscription outweighed the benefits of people like him holding Fellowships.[2] He therefore resigned from his Fellowship position in May 1869 (though he was soon after rehired in a (much less well compensated) position not requiring subscription; he regained his Fellowship in 1885). It was while thinking about his ethical dilemma that he developed many of the ideas that he recorded in *The Methods of Ethics*. As he explains,

> I did my very best to decide the question [of whether it was permissible to retain his Fellowship despite his doubts] methodically on general principles, but I found it very difficult, and I may say that it was while struggling with this difficulty thence arising that I went through a good deal of the thought that was ultimately systematised in the *Methods of Ethics*. (M 38)

What emerged from this thinking is a rich philosophical harvest, worthy of study for three reasons.

First, the *Methods* clarifies and tackles some of the most enduring and difficult problems of morality. It offers readers a high-calibre example of analytical moral philosophy. It is, as John Rawls states in the Foreword to the Hackett edition of *The Method of Ethics*, the "first truly academic work in moral philosophy which undertakes to provide a systematic comparative study of moral conceptions, starting with those which historically and by present assessment are the most significant" (ME v).

Second, the *Methods* provides a distinct defence of utilitarianism. The result of this is, as Rawls points out (again in the Foreword), "the clearest and most accessible formulation" of classical utilitarianism developed in light of a comprehensive understanding of the difficulties the view faces and how to remedy them in a way that does not involve deserting its core commitments (ME v).

Third, unlike his other works, the *Methods* continues to inspire contemporary philosophers to a significant degree. Derek Parfit says it is the "best book on ethics ever written ... [containing] the largest number of true and important claims" (Parfit, 2011: xxxiii).[3] Sidgwick's work inspires because in addition to

---

[2] For the full argument, see Sidgwick 1870.

[3] For a similar view, see Broad, 1930: 143; Smart, 1956: 347; Crisp, 2015: vii. In contrast, Elizabeth Anscombe says she finds Sidgwick a "dull author" who shows a "corrupt mind" (Anscombe, 1958: 10, 17).

its distinct defence of utilitarianism, the *Methods* includes arguments for a range of normative and meta-ethical positions worthy of careful consideration and (in many cases) defence.

Despite all this, the *Methods* has a reputation (even amongst admirers like Parfit) for being heavy going and at times dull and boring. The book is certainly not kind to its readers: it's ineffectively organized, densely written and long. It requires patience and effort to grasp its main and most influential arguments. It therefore presents a challenge to readers. In part the function of this Element is to guide readers through some of the work's most important and influential arguments.

Bernard Williams provides a helpful way of viewing the book. He agrees with others that the *Methods* is at times dull and boring, but, he rightly points out, not all of it is boring, for "distinct moments of tension . . . grow out of passages of that very boredom" (Williams, 1995: 156). Williams fruitfully likens the *Methods* to a cricket match:

> One might say indeed that the overwhelming Englishness of this book extends even to a similarity to a cricket match, which has the very sophisticated feature that one can appreciate the significant detail of the monotony that lies before one at a given time only because one understands remote and hypothetical moments of excitement that might grow from it. (Williams, 1995: 156)

Sidgwick's Ethics explores three signal and influential instances of tension and excitement in the *Methods*, including:

1. Sidgwick's argument that our common-sense morality comprising norms like keep your promises and refrain from lying is a theoretically unsatisfactory method of ethical reasoning.
2. Sidgwick's distinctive argument that utilitarianism, the view that one ought only to maximize general happiness, is a compelling method of ethical reasoning.
3. Sidgwick's argument that rational egoism, the view that one ought only to maximize one's own surplus happiness, is no less compelling than utilitarianism as a method of ethical reasoning and that, because the two views at times offer coordinate but conflicting verdicts in practice, there exists a dualism of practical reason.

These are among Sidgwick's lasting contributions to ethics and why the *Methods* is one of the most influential works in the history of moral philosophy and merits careful study. No other work of Sidgwick's has comparable significance, though some other works (relied on here) help to shed light on the views he defends in the *Methods*. It is hoped that this exploration will contribute to establishing which of Sidgwick's claims are true and important and to determining whether his mind is, as Anscombe says (1958: 17), "corrupt" (and, if so, how).

This Element has five main sections. Section 1 acquaints readers with the focus of *The Methods of Ethics*. Section 2 discusses Sidgwick's approach to moral justification – intuitionism – which is central to his critical attack on common-sense morality and his argument for utilitarianism. Section 3 examines Sidgwick's rejection of common-sense morality, focusing on the duty of veracity. Section 4 explores Sidgwick's argument for utilitarianism. Section 5 clarifies his argument for rational egoism and the structure of the dualism of practical reason.

1 The *Methods*

Sidgwick begins the *Methods* by defining a method of ethics as "any rational procedure by which we determine what individual human beings 'ought'– or what it is 'right' for them – to do, or to seek to realize by voluntary action" (ME 1). A method of ethics offers a mechanism for figuring out what we ought, all things considered, to do in any particular situation.

Three methods of ethics receive sustained treatment:

1. Rational egoism, which holds that

    the rational agent regards quantity of consequent pleasure and pain to himself as alone important in choosing between alternatives of action; and seeks always the greatest attainable surplus of pleasure over pain – which . . . we may designate as his 'greatest happiness.' (ME 95; also 121)

2. Dogmatic intuitionism, which says that

    certain kinds of actions are right and reasonable in themselves, apart from their consequences; – or rather with a merely partial consideration of consequences, from which other consequences admitted to be possibly good or bad are definitely excluded. (ME 200; also 312–3, 337; PC 564–5; GSM 159)

Dogmatic intuitionism includes obligations of beneficence, promise-keeping, justice, and veracity. Some of these obligations restrict the means we may take to obtain our goals and rest in part on backward-looking considerations. For example, if we have previously made a promise, it is in itself right to keep it even when it might be slightly more beneficial to break it.

3. Utilitarianism, which maintains that

    the conduct which, under any given circumstances, is objectively right, is that which will produce the greatest amount of happiness on the whole; that is, taking into account all whose happiness is affected by the conduct. (ME 411)[4]

The *Methods* comprises four Books. Sidgwick clarifies and evaluates the foregoing methods in Books II, III, and IV, respectively. Book I clarifies, among other

---

[4] By the "greatest amount of happiness on the whole" Sidgwick means the "greatest possible surplus of pleasure over pain" (ME 413).

things, his meta-ethics and his moral epistemology, elements of which we shall touch on below. Our focus now is on what motivates Sidgwick's inquiry.

People persistently ask, Sidgwick says, why should I do what I see to be right? He thinks the best explanation of the question's persistence is that in reasoning about what to do common people appeal to a "loose combination or confusion of methods" (ME 102). The common person relies, that is, on a plurality of principles and methods in her ethical deliberation (ME 5–6). She believes it is right, for example, to keep her promises, tell the truth and promote her own and general happiness. However, the common person does not relate these principles or methods to each other systematically: "the unphilosophic … [person] is apt to hold different principles at once, and to apply different methods in more or less confused combination" (ME 6).

This leaves the common person in many situations in which she has to decide what to do without clarity respecting the relative importance of the principles she holds and therefore of what it is right all things considered to do. She has made a promise to give more to charity but soon realizes that keeping the promise will mean forgoing significant benefits for her and her family. She consequently wonders what is right for her to do given there are many actions in any one circumstance she believes to have the characteristic of being right (ME 5). She wonders what, all things considered, is it right to do given the diversity of things in any one situation appearing to be right.

At this point the moral philosopher enters the fray. She "seeks unity of principle, and consistency of method" (ME 6; PE 31–2). She supplies a unified and systematic moral framework. This provides an account of what matters to the morality of an action and a mechanism for rationally balancing all morally relevant considerations against one another and delivering clarity respecting what all things considered we ought to do (ME viii). The philosopher differs from the common person in assuming that

> [w]e cannot … regard as valid reasonings that lead to conflicting conclu-
> sions; and … therefore assume[s] as a fundamental postulate of Ethics, that
> so far as two methods conflict, one or other of them must be modified or
> rejected. (ME 6; also 12)

Following Kant, Sidgwick distinguishes between hypothetical and categorical oughts (Kant, 2002: 4:413–14). Hypothetical oughts are conditional on the existence of a desire one has. The claim you ought to catch the 15:15 train from London to Toronto binds you only if you desire to be in Toronto by 18:00. Categorical oughts are not conditional on the existence of a desire one has. They oblige regardless of one's desires. You ought to keep your promises whether or not you desire to do so. The three methods Sidgwick focuses on prescribe categorical oughts: oughts prescribed "without any tacit assumption of a still ulterior end" (ME 7).

Sidgwick focuses on dogmatic intuitionism, rational egoism, and utilitarianism because each, he thinks, "the common sense of mankind is *prima facie* prepared to accept as ultimate" (ME 6; also 12). Two ends are, he adds, widely accepted as ultimately rational (non-instrumentally good), happiness (pleasure) and perfection (the development of essential human mental capacities (moral and intellectual) to a high degree) (ME 9). He explores hedonistic versions of egoism and utilitarianism. But he does not investigate perfectionist versions of egoism and utilitarianism. Why not?

Consider:

> Perfectionist egoism: An agent is rational insofar as she maximises her own perfection (i.e., insofar as she realises her essential human mental qualities to an excellent or ideal degree).

> Pluralistic egoism: An agent is rational insofar as she maximises her own happiness and her own perfection.

Sidgwick ignores perfectionist egoism because, he says, perfectionist egoism *prima facie* coincides with dogmatic intuitionism to a great extent (ME 11; 83–4). The coincidence claim rests on two further claims: that acting virtuously (or exercising the mental capacities that are moral in nature) is the most valuable element of perfection, preferable to any other element of perfection with which it might compete, and that to act virtuously is equivalent to acting in accordance with dogmatic intuitionism (telling the truth, keeping promises, etc.).

Both claims seem contestable, however. First, it seems plausible that it is rational, at least in some cases, for one to forgo a very small amount of one's virtue to gain a much greater amount of some other (intellectual) perfection for oneself (e.g., rational activity in scholarly pursuits). If there are forms of egoistic perfectionism on which virtue is not always the most valuable element of human perfection, there are forms of the view that do not coincide with dogmatic intuitionism. Room is then left for versions of perfectionist egoism distinguishable from dogmatic intuitionism and (potentially) worth taking seriously on their own.

Second, it is not clear why Sidgwick thinks virtue involves acting in accordance with dogmatic intuitionism rather than, say, utilitarianism or some other view. At the very least an argument needs to be provided to the effect that reasoning as a dogmatic intuitionist is what virtue (for the perfectionist) involves. In reply, Sidgwick might suggest that even if it is true that virtue comprised utilitarianism instead of dogmatic intuitionism perfectionist egoism would still not lead to a distinct method, since the egoistic perfectionist would reason as a utilitarian (a method Sidgwick explores), and so there would be no need to provide egoistic perfectionism with separate treatment.

This reply does not adequately explain why Sidgwick takes the putative coincidence of perfectionist egoism with other methods he explores as a reason against exploring perfectionist egoism separately. He says utilitarianism and dogmatic intuitionism ultimately coincide (at least roughly speaking), but he provides them with separate treatment. His thought must be that while utilitarianism and dogmatic intuitionism coincide, separate treatment of them is warranted because despite the coincidence the two views involve quite distinct modes of moral reasoning. Separate treatment of dogmatic intuitionism and perfectionist egoism (with virtue as the most important element of perfection) would not, by contrast, be warranted, since they do not involve distinct forms of moral reasoning. However, one might wonder in response whether Sidgwick is entitled to submit this in advance of any such separate treatment. Dogmatic intuitionism and perfectionist egoism may have (and are likely to have), for example, distinct ways of reasoning about how to reconcile the conflicts that occur between the main principles of common-sense morality.

As to pluralistic egoism Sidgwick seems to think that on the whole pluralistic views of this sort are to be eschewed (ME 95). He thinks monistic views are preferable, even though endorsing them leads to "paradox," or conflict with common-sense morality (ME 6; FC 383). He provides little in the way of argument for his (controversial) preference.

Let's turn to utilitarian versions of perfectionism.

> Perfectionist utilitarianism: An agent acts rightly insofar as she performs the action that, out of the range of actions open to her, maximises aggregate perfection.

> Pluralistic utilitarianism: An agent acts rightly insofar as she performs the action that, out of the range of actions open to her, maximises both perfection and happiness for the aggregate.

Sidgwick rejects the former view because no moralist has ever "approved" of an individual sacrificing their own moral perfection to promote the greater perfection of others (ME 11). Sidgwick agrees some moralists have approved of or might approve of an individual sacrificing some of their own non-moral (intellectual) perfection to promote a greater quantity of surplus non-moral or moral perfection for others. His concern lies with moral perfection or the mental qualities manifested in virtuous action. No moralist, he says, has "approved" of an individual sacrificing her own *moral excellence* or *perfection* – part of perfection – to promote another's greater moral perfection or excellence.

Sidgwick does not really tell us why it might be impermissible to sacrifice one's own virtue in order to promote the greater virtue of another. He is not here worried about uncompensated sacrifice. Worries of this kind would speak against considering hedonistic utilitarianism which, Sidgwick well knows, demands uncompensated sacrifice (ME 498, 87; FC 483). The view he is reporting seems to be that there is something special about one's own moral excellence or perfection making it inappropriate to sacrifice it but no other goods, perfectionist or otherwise, for the greater benefit of others.

But it is not obviously inappropriate to sacrifice one's own moral excellence to promote greater moral excellence. If it is not inappropriate, there might be room for perfectionist utilitarianism.

Consider:

> White Lie 1: Suppose I tell myself a small lie in order to make it true that I will be significantly more virtuous in the future. Imagine the lie provides me with a long-lasting kind of positive affect making me more likely to consider and act on moral considerations.

I sacrifice my present virtue for a greater gain in my future virtue. It seems permissible for me to lie to myself. But if it is okay to sacrifice virtue in this case, why not in others?

Consider:

> White Lie 2: Suppose Jones is about to harm several people with some scandalous lies. I can lie to Jones and tell him he looks good in his suit when he does not. Suppose the positive affective boost Jones gets from my lie disposes him to choose for good reasons not to tell the scandalous lies.

If the lie really is small, you might think the small loss of my virtue is worth the gain in Jones' virtue. One might reply that in this case I do not really sacrifice my virtue. Because I make the world on balance more virtuous I therefore qualify as virtuous. But this merely dismisses or rules out the main element of the (puzzling) view Sidgwick considers, that each has a reason relative to them to promote their own virtue.

Sidgwick dismisses pluralistic utilitarianism because it leads to irresolvable conflicts. He endorses hedonism – the view that only pleasure (pain) has non-instrumental (dis)value – in part because it provides a way to rationally compare the value of and to reconcile conflicts between competing aims (knowledge, freedom, contemplation of beauty, and so on) (ME 406). The arguments against the pluralist views are an indication of the strong brand of systematicity that Sidgwick relies on but never argues for. It seems too strong.

When discussing the two different methods derivable from taking happiness as the ultimate categorically prescribed end, Sidgwick suggests it is

> possible to adopt an end intermediate between the two, and to aim at the happiness of some limited portion of mankind, such as one's family or nation or race: but any such limitation seems arbitrary, and probably few would maintain it to be reasonable *per se*, except as the most practicable way of aiming at the general happiness, or of indirectly securing one's own. (ME 10)

Sidgwick might be right about arbitrariness if what he has in mind is a view stating, for example, that only one's family's happiness matters or only one's co-nationals' happiness counts. It seems hard to justify limitations of this kind. However, what about a view saying everyone's happiness matters, but not to the same degree, in reasoning about what to do? My family's happiness might have a greater claim on me than the happiness of strangers, for example. On this view, the scope of morality would be broad, but its weighting variable. This view is not without its attractions, though Sidgwick does not directly address it. It is unclear that the views he goes on to defend – utilitarianism and egoism – can support this view in a plausible way.

Sidgwick says his aim in the *Methods* is not "any such complete and final solution of the chief ethical difficulties and controversies as would convert this exposition of various methods into the development of a harmonious system" (ME 13; also vi; SE 411). However, he provides a detailed argument against dogmatic intuitionism, a distinctive argument in favour of utilitarianism which emerges in part from his dissatisfaction with common-sense morality, and he concludes the *Methods* arguing that rational egoism and utilitarianism appear as equally plausible yet rival and conflicting conceptions of what we have most reason to do, and therefore there is a "Dualism of Practical Reason" (ME 496–509; UG 30–1; SE 411; FC 483–7).

It is far from clear, then, that Sidgwick discusses the methods of ethics that he considers merely in order to "point out their mutual relations; and where they seem to conflict, to define the issue as much as possible" (ME 14). He expresses (as we have seen) firm views about which methods merit sustained investigation and he advocates for certain theses.

This section discussed the general focus of Sidgwick's *Methods*. The next section discusses Sidgwick's intuitionism and the epistemic tests he applies to propositions appearing to be self-evident.

2 Sidgwick's Intuitionism

Sidgwick describes the *Methods* as involving the search for knowledge of the methods for reaching conclusions about what we ought to do, morally speaking, rather than knowledge of the "practical results to which our methods lead" (ME viii; cf. 215). The aim of this inquiry is "systematic and precise general knowledge of what ought to be" (ME 1). This inquiry qualifies as ethical philosophy because its primary concern is "the general principles and methods of moral reasoning" (PSR 25).

Sidgwick's main focus in the *Methods* is methods of reasoning about what we ought to do, which, it is important to note, comprises thinking about the correct principles on which such reasoning relies. Hence, Sidgwick's reference above to principles and methods. Each of the methods of ethics he explores is committed to at least one principle.

One question immediately arising is this: How are such principles known? Sidgwick thinks our knowledge of principles depends (at least in part) on intuition:

> It should ... be observed that the current contrast between 'intuitive' or '*a priori*' and 'inductive' or '*a posteriori*' morality commonly involves a certain confusion of thought. For what the 'inductive' moralist professes to know by induction, is commonly not the same thing as what the 'intuitive' moralist professes to know by intuition. In the former case it is the conduciveness to pleasure of certain kinds of action that is methodologically ascertained: in the latter case, their rightness: there is therefore no proper opposition. If Hedonism claims to give authoritative guidance, this can only be in virtue of the principle that pleasure is the only reasonable ultimate end of human action: and this principle cannot be known by induction from experience. Experience can at most tell us that all men always do seek pleasure as their ultimate end ... it cannot tell us that anyone ought so to seek it. If this latter proposition is legitimately affirmed in respect either of private or of general happiness, it must either be immediately known to be true, – and therefore, we may say, a moral intuition – or be inferred ultimately from premises which include at least one such moral intuition; hence either species of Hedonism, regarded from the point of view primarily taken in this treatise, might be legitimately said to be in a certain sense 'intuitional'. It seems, however, to be the prevailing opinion of ordinary moral persons, and of most of the writers who have maintained the existence of moral intuitions, that certain kinds of actions are unconditionally prescribed without regard to ulterior consequences: and I have accordingly treated this doctrine as a distinguishing characteristic of the [Dogmatic] Intuitional method, during the main part of the detailed examination of that method which I attempt in Book iii. (ME 97–8; also 201; PC 564)

Sidgwick is thus an intuitionist. Accordingly, he holds that knowledge of basic moral principles is direct or non-inferential (ME 201, 383; PC 564; FC 484). Sidgwick thinks the moral truths knowable in this way are self-evident. A self-evident proposition is such that a proper understanding of its terms is sufficient to warrant one accepting it (ME 229, 379).

Sidgwick distinguishes between narrow and wide intuitionism (ME 120n1, 201). Intuitionism in the wide sense comprises the above epistemological view: first principles "if known at all must be intuitively known" (ME 201). This is the sense in which Sidgwick is an intuitionist. He aims, as we shall see, to show the basis of utilitarianism "could only be supplied by a fundamental intuition" (ME xxii–xxiii; also PC 564).

Intuitionism in the narrow sense is equivalent to dogmatic intuitionism, which combines wide or epistemological intuitionism with the normative position that there is a plurality of basic general rules rooted in common-sense morality (which he mentions at the end of the quoted paragraph and about which more momentarily).

Sidgwick is not explicit about why he endorses epistemic intuitionism. The only place in which he appears to offer an argument for the view is in the long passage quoted above.[5] The first premise involves a commitment to the claim that we cannot infer ought from is (non-trivially). Sidgwick's commitment to this claim is clear.

> From the mere knowledge that a certain result is what will be or preponderantly tends to be, it is impossible to infer that it ought to be. (IO 90; also CNSE 585–6; FP 107; ME 98; PE 68; PSR 237; SE 412)

The second premise of the argument involves a commitment to foundationalism about knowledge, the view that there exist basic and non-basic beliefs. The former are non-inferentially warranted while the latter are inferentially warranted by appeal to the former.

From these premises Sidgwick seems to conclude that if moral propositions are known (or justified), they are either known directly or non-inferentially or known indirectly or inferentially on the basis of an inference from at least one moral proposition known directly or non-inferentially. Hence, intuitionism.

Sidgwick does not explicitly consider alternatives to intuitionism. However, one prominent alternative to intuitionism is coherentism, which holds that the justification of beliefs is a matter of the relations between them. Coherentism involves the denial that there are non-inferentially warranted propositions. It holds that a moral belief is justified insofar as it is a member of a coherent belief set. A belief set's coherence relations are a matter of, among other things, the logical, probabilistic, and explanatory relations existing between its members.

Before saying more about Sidgwick's brand of intuitionism it is important to note that he thinks intuition is *fallible*:

---

[5] For detailed discussion of this paragraph, see Phillips, 2011: 53–8.

by calling any affirmation as to the rightness or wrongness of actions "intuitive," I do not mean to prejudge the question as to its ultimate validity, when philosophically considered: I only mean that its truth is apparently known immediately, and not as the result of reasoning. I admit the possibility that any such "intuition" may turn out to have an element of error, which subsequent reflection and comparison may enable us to correct. (ME 211; also PC 565)

Sidgwick's view, then, is that an intuition that X is wrong does not entail that X is wrong. It entails only that X *appears* wrong. It might, on reflection, emerge that X is not wrong. Intuition is therefore fallible. It is important to keep this in mind as we are thinking about Sidgwick's treatment of dogmatic intuitionism.

One of the tasks Sidgwick sets for himself is to determine which intuitions to accept and which to reject. To accomplish this task, he seeks to determine whether any of them

> possess the characteristics by which self-evident truths are distinguished from mere opinions. (ME 338)

Determining this involves, for Sidgwick, appealing to

> four conditions, the complete fulfilment of which would establish a significant proposition, apparently self-evident, in the highest degree of certainty attainable. (ME 338)

It is important to explicate the function of Sidgwick's four conditions. In his work in epistemology, he applies similar conditions to intuitions generally. It is not possible, he says, to find criteria *guaranteeing* intuitive truth (LK 461). Instead, we have only criteria "*useful* ... as a means of guarding against error" rather than infallibly indicating intuitive truth (LK 461). When a proposition apparently known immediately satisfies the conditions its truth is not guaranteed. We have shown only that we have done the utmost to exclude error based on experience of the ways in which humans have detected and been then "led to discard it" (LK 466).[6]

Sidgwick's four conditions state

1. "The terms of the proposition must be clear and precise" (ME 338).

This condition claims that we may avoid error in an intuition by ensuring that its content and the practical implications of it are clear and precise.[7] Clarity and

---

[6] For discussion of Sidgwick's conditions, see Shaver, 1999: 62–74; Irwin, 2009: 489–90; Skelton, 2010: 495–6; Phillips, 2011: 60–2; Hurka 2014b: 112–17.

[7] See, e.g., Crisp, 2002: 70; Phillips, 2011: 101 for the claim that this condition demands clear and precise practical guidance; for doubts, see de Lazari-Radek and Singer, 2014: 144–8. Sidgwick seems to insist on clear and precise practical guidance. For example, Sidgwick faults the intuition that we ought to keep our promises on the grounds that it does not tell us what to do in a range of cases (ME 353–4).

precision in propositions judged self-evident is one way in which to avoid the error in intuitions revealed by conflict between a judgement "first formed" and the view of this judgement "taken by the same mind on subsequent reconsideration" (LK 466).

2. "The self-evidence of the proposition must be ascertained by careful reflection" (ME 339).

Conducting this test is important because

> most persons are liable to confound intuitions, on the one hand with mere impressions or impulses, which to careful observation do not present themselves as claiming to be dictates of Reason; and on the other hand, with mere opinions, to which the familiarity that comes from frequent hearing and repetition often gives a false appearance of self-evidence which attentive reflection disperses. (ME 339)

In his work in epistemology, he says this condition might help us see if "we had mistaken for an intuition what was merely inference or belief accepted on authority" (LK 462). He remarks on this in the *Methods* when he discusses the existence and validity of intuitions. He says whether we have intuitions is to be decided by "direct introspection or reflection" (ME 211). He insists this is no small matter. Intuitions are liable to be confounded with

> blind impulses to certain kinds of action or vague sentiments of preference for them, or conclusions from rapid and half-unconscious processes of reasoning, or current opinions to which familiarity has given an illusory air of self-evidence. (ME 211–12)

The purpose of this condition is to determine by means of focused reflection the existence of an intuition by ensuring that its source is rational and a matter of self-evidence (not authority or familiarity). This test is useful for segregating intuitions from beliefs problematically based solely on external authority or having their origin in strong sentiment.

3. "The propositions accepted as self-evident must be mutually consistent" (ME 341).

This test matters, since conflict between intuitions implies "there is error in one or the other, or in both" intuitions (ME 341). For Sidgwick, the relevant conflicts are between intuitions (and their implications) rather than between intuitions and beliefs of any kind (LK 462–3). Sidgwick is clear in the *Methods* and in his epistemological writings that the conditions concern "intuitions" only (*pace* Shaver, 1999: 65–7). In the latter, he describes this test – a form of discursive verification – as involving an attempt to remove error in our intuitions by carefully grouping the *intuitions* that we see to be related, and surveying them together in the most systematic order possible. (LK 462–3; emphasis added)

A conflict between intuitions suggests that we may have "mistaken for an ultimate and independent axiom one that is really derivative and subordinate" (ME 341). It is important to see this test as helping to discover error that the previous introspective or reflective tests, which focus on intuitions in isolation, may fail to detect.

4. The propositions accepted as self-evident must not be denied by someone of whom I have no more reason to suspect of being in error than I am.

Sidgwick maintains

> denial by another of a proposition that I have affirmed has a tendency to impair my confidence in its validity. (ME 341)

By "another" he here means one equally or more "competent to judge" or "expert" (ME xxxiv; LK 464, 466), that is, one I believe is no more likely to be in error than I am. The condition seemingly requires that if there is conflict between what I intuit and what another intuits my confidence in my intuition should decrease, unless I have reason to suspect it is more likely error is in the other (dissenting) mind than in my own (ME 342; LK 465), for "if I have no more reason to suspect error in the other mind than my own, reflective comparison between the two judgements necessarily reduces me temporarily to a state of neutrality" (ME 342).

Or, as he puts it elsewhere:

> It is obvious that in any such conflict [between rival intuitors] there must be error on one side or the other, or on both. The natural man will often decide unhesitatingly that the error is on the other side. But it is manifest that a philosophic mind cannot do this, unless it can prove independently that the conflicting intuitor has an inferior faculty of envisaging truth in general or this kind of truth; one who cannot do this must reasonably submit to a loss of confidence in any intuition of his own that thus is found to conflict with another's. (LK 464)

There is one noteworthy difference between what Sidgwick says in this passage (from his work on epistemology) and what he says in the *Methods*. In the passage just quoted, he says that expert disagreement with an intuition one affirms ought to reduce one's confidence in it. In the *Methods* he says that expert disagreement (it seems) ought to reduce one to a state of neutrality between one's intuition and the intuition of another competent to judge (Crisp, 2015: 110). Loss of confidence and a state of neutrality are not the same. He does not mention neutrality in his epistemological writings and he mentions neutrality only once in the *Methods*. He seems later in the *Methods* to opt for the view that expert disagreement ought only to reduce one's confidence in an intuition. In discussing the intuitions he endorses (outlined below), he says he "should" rely less confidently on them had "those moralists . . . most in earnest in seeking . . . genuine intuitions" not agreed on them (ME 384). He does not say he would be or should be reduced to a state of neutrality considering such disagreement.

Sidgwick seems to maintain that his tests are for self-evidence or self-evident truth. They are to determine, it seems, whether a proposition really is self-evident. The thought, then, is that an intuition or putative self-evident proposition surviving the tests or possessing the conditions is the closest we can approximate to authentic self-evident truth (Skelton, 2010). The purpose of the tests is to determine whether an initial intuition we have survives rigorous scrutiny.

However, it has been suggested that Sidgwick is not interested only in establishing self-evidence. The aim of the application of the four conditions is not to test for self-evidence or self-evident truth alone but to establish higher certainties (Shaver, 1999: 64–5; Phillips, 2011: 61–2, 78, 86n9; Crisp, 2015: 108n21). This view relies on a particular understanding of Sidgwick's tests or conditions. On the clearest version of this understanding, conditions 1 and 2 above are concerned with establishing self-evidence or that one has a bona fide intuition or self-evident proposition, while conditions 3 and 4 are concerned with establishing whether such a self-evident proposition has further (inferential) support and therefore qualifies as a higher certainty. A proposition that qualifies as a higher certainty, then, is actually apparently known non-derivatively *and* supported by consistency with other propositions that one apparently knows non-derivatively and by consensus with others competent to judge. On this account, apparently self-evident propositions (propositions passing tests 1 and 2) have their warrant enhanced through relations with other (self-evident) propositions (test 3) and through agreement from competent judges (test 4). Such propositions would qualify as higher certainties.

True, Sidgwick often writes as though his aim in using the tests is not to establish higher certainties but, instead, to segregate real self-evidence from apparent self-evidence.[8] He says, for example, that he uses the tests to establish self-evident propositions and to distinguish these from "mere opinions" (ME 338). However, the position that he is on the hunt for higher certainties has both textual support and philosophical merit.

---

[8] For this point and discussion of Sidgwick's lack of clarity, see Hurka, 2014b: 112–14.

Sidgwick says that he is, along with other philosophers, looking for "moral propositions . . . [that are] certain *and* self-evident" (ME 374; emphasis added). He notes in addition that

> A proposition which presents itself to my mind as self-evident, and is in harmony with all the rest of my intuitions relating to the same subject, and is also ascertained to be accepted by all other minds that have been led to contemplate it, may after all turn out to be false: but it seems to have as high a degree of certainty as I can hope to attain under the existing conditions of human thought. (FP 109)

This suggests that he is searching for more than self-evidence. Moreover, in his epistemological writings Sidgwick suggests test 3 introduces the value of system (LK 463, 467). In this context, he mentions coherence (LK 466). Sidgwick might think that when clear and precise intuitions ascertained by reflection cohere with each other their certainty is enhanced. True, he does not say this in the *Methods*. His focus there is on consistency and he does not clearly mention consistency between intuitions enhancing justification.[9] Sidgwick's focus is on how inconsistency may undermine a proposition's claim to self-evidence (ME 341). Inconsistency is a way of discovering error that reflection on intuitions in isolation may fail to reveal. This may, however, not be a decisive reason to reject the thought that, for Sidgwick, if two propositions considered self-evident after the application of tests 1 and 2 stand consistent with each other, the certainty of each is at least to some extent amplified or enhanced. He seems to suggest at places outside the *Methods* as we have just seen that harmony amongst ethical intuitions increases their certainty (FP 109; LK 465).[10]

In his discussion of test 4, Sidgwick seems to say satisfying it provides support for propositions considered self-evident (ME xxxiv, 384). Passing the fourth test might increase the certainty of one's intuition by removing reasons for doubt (FP 109). So if after applying the first three tests you consider it self-evident that you ought to promote the good, the absence of disagreement with experts might enhance its warrant by further excluding possible sources of doubt potentially revealed by those conditions.

We must here, note, not conflate agreement with experts with agreement with common-sense morality.[11] Receiving support for an intuition from competent

---

[9] For discussion, see Skelton, 2010: 496.

[10] Sidgwick's focus in the *Methods* is exclusively on the consistency of apparently self-evident propositions with each other. It does not seem plausible that, for Sidgwick, consistency with common-sense morality amplifies the certainty of an apparently self-evident proposition (contra Shaver, 1999: 65–7 and Phillips, 2011: 79–80; for discussion, see Skelton, 2010).

[11] For this conflation, see Shaver, 1999: 65–6; Phillips, 2011: 79–80. Sidgwick may seem concerned in places to demonstrate that the plain man agrees with what he takes to be self-evident (ME 382). It is not clear, however, that his considered view is that the plain person is a competent

judges is not the same as receiving support from common sense. When Sidgwick appeals to agreement amongst experts in support of his philosophical intuitions (discussed below), he appeals to philosophers (ME 384). He is clear in his discussion of the philosophical intuitions that he has transcended common-sense morality and is telling the plain person what she ought to think (ME 373).

If tests 3 and 4 function to enhance the certainty of apparently self-evident propositions, then Sidgwick's tests as a whole will have to be understood as establishing not just self-evidence but (something like) higher certainties. Higher certainty, on this understanding, will involve determining clarity and precision (test 1), ascertaining apparent self-evidence (test 2), consistency between the apparently self-evident propositions one accepts (test 3), and lack of dissensus from or consistency with the intuitions of others no more likely to be in error than oneself (test 4).

The tests, then, seek to determine whether a claim initially thought to be self-evident – you ought to tell the truth – is a higher certainty.

In this section, we discussed Sidgwick's intuitionism and the tests he applies to establish higher certainties. Sidgwick's epistemology appeals to both self-evidence and relations between beliefs to establish such certainties. He seems to give a role, then, to elements of foundationalism and coherentism. In the next section, we will explore one example of Sidgwick's treatment of the main principles of dogmatic intuitionism (or common-sense morality).

3 Dogmatic Intuitionism and Its Infelicities

Sidgwick has two goals in his treatment of dogmatic intuitionism. His first is to isolate the main rules of common-sense morality claimed to be intuitively known and to clarify their content. His second is to determine whether such intuitions "can claim to be classed as Intuitive Truths" (ME 343) or "stand the test of rigorous examination" (ME 462).

Let's start with what Sidgwick says about particular intuitions. A familiar feature of moral life involves passing moral judgement on particular actions. We are certain of the morality of some. When Meera lies to Ali merely to entice him to help her with her gardening project, we seem confident Meera acts wrongly.

We are conflicted in some cases. Tracy and Sam are friends. Sam is taking it easy in life. He is uninterested in developing his talents. Tracy thinks, on the one hand, as Sam's friend, that she should pressure him to develop his talents. But

---

judge or expert given the sound trashing he delivers to common-sense morality. For a discussion of the role of appeals to common-sense morality in Sidgwick, see Skelton 2010.

Tracy holds, on the other hand, she should respect Sam's choices. Tracy is unable to decide the conflict. She goes back and forth on what to do.

We are puzzled in other cases. Bob is good friends with Ted and Tony, who have been a couple for many years. Ted and Tony have decided to separate. Bob likes Ted and Tony and wants to support them both. But Bob is not sure, of the ways of doing so, which is right.

Sidgwick thinks we have intuitions about particular cases (ME 99–100). We seem to know directly that Meera is treating Ali wrongly. But he agrees there are cases of the sort Tracy and Bob find themselves in, where we are uncertain of what to do, morally speaking, and there is the distinct possibility of making an error in judgement. As Sidgwick notes,

> in any concrete case the complexity of circumstances necessarily increases the difficulty of judging, and our personal interests or habitual sympathies are liable to disturb the clearness of our moral discernment. (ME 214; also 100)

Sidgwick thinks we might avoid errors or gaps in our intuitions about particular cases by appeal to "general rules or formulae" (ME 214):

> Only exceptionally confident persons find that they always seem to see clearly what ought to be done in any case that comes before them. Most of us, however unhesitatingly we may affirm rightness and wrongness in ordinary matters of conduct, yet not unfrequently meet with cases where our unreasoned judgement fails us; and where we could no more decide the moral issue raised without appealing to some general formula, than we could decide a disputed legal claim without reference to the positive law that deals with the matter. (ME 214)

Sidgwick locates a plurality of such general rules by "a little reflection and observation of men's moral discourse" (ME 214). When this set of rules is "regarded as a body of moral truth, warranted to be such by the *consensus* of mankind ... it is ... termed the morality of Common Sense" (ME 215; also 100). The morality of common sense includes general obligations of wisdom, of beneficence, of justice, of promise-keeping, and of veracity. It might be possible to appeal to these to avoid errors or gaps in our judgements or intuitions about particular cases.

Sidgwick focuses on the main rules of common-sense morality in *Methods* Book III. The dogmatic intuitionist attempts to arrange the morality of common sense "as systematically as possible, and by proper definitions and explanations to remove vagueness and prevent conflict" (ME 101; also 215). Sidgwick endeavours to determine what these rules involve when clearly and precisely rendered and whether they may serve as the most basic requirements of morality.

Dogmatic intuitionism, recall, says we (rational agents) have

> the power of seeing clearly that certain kinds of actions are right and reason-
> able in themselves, apart from their consequences; – or rather with a merely
> partial consideration of consequences, from which other consequences
> admitted to be possibly good or bad are definitely excluded. (ME 200; also
> 98, 312–13, 337)

Dogmatic intuitionism – a brand of deontology – includes several commitments worth distinguishing clearly. First, it subscribes to a plurality of general formulae (e.g., keep your promises, tell the truth, and distribute happiness according to merit). Second, these formulae restrict or constrain the means we may take to desirable ends (e.g., general happiness): even if you can produce slightly more happiness by lying than by telling the truth, you ought not to lie. Third, it rests our obligations in part on retrospective considerations. When I consider the obligation that I have to pay my debt to you my focus is (in part) on the fact that in the past I have incurred a debt to you. Our obligations depend not only on what will happen but what has happened. Fourth, as we have already noted, these general formulae, it is claimed, may be known directly on the basis of reflection.

The first three commitments express normative positions. In embracing these, dogmatic intuitionism distinguishes itself from rational egoism and utilitarianism. The latter agree one ought, at bottom, to promote happiness, but disagree on whose happiness to promote. Egoists maintain one ought to advance only one's own happiness. Utilitarians hold one ought to advance only aggregate happiness. Both reject self-standing constraints or restrictions on the means we take to the promotion of happiness, pluralism about moral principles, and that our obligations rest (even in part) on retrospective considerations. The fourth commitment of dogmatic intuitionism, as noted, is epistemological, and may be agreed to by both egoism and utilitarianism.

Sidgwick dissects all the main rules of common-sense morality. In this section, we focus on his clarification of the obligation of veracity. A firm grasp of Sidgwick's treatment of such an obligation is required for understanding his endorsement of utilitarianism, which emerges (in part) from his dissatisfaction with common-sense morality as a method.

Sidgwick discusses the obligation of veracity in *Methods* Book III, ch. vii. The duty of veracity requires, he says, that we "utter words" which we believe will have the effect of producing "in other minds beliefs corresponding to our own" (ME 314). This may be hard in some cases, for example, where the meaning of certain phrases – for example, I am busy – is degraded. But in most cases conveying one's beliefs to others is not hard. And Sidgwick says

> many moralists have regarded this, from its simplicity and definiteness, as
> a quite unexceptionable instance of an ethical axiom [intuitive truth]. (ME 315)

The question, then, is whether the duty of veracity is an absolute and independent moral requirement constraining what may be done as a means to promoting happiness or well-being.

Sidgwick's assessment begins by noting that common sense is not exactly clear whether the duty of veracity is absolute and "needing no further justification" (ME 315). The advocate of common sense might agree only with:

> it is merely a general right of each man to have truth spoken to him by his fellows. (ME 315)

In this case, the duty of veracity is not plausibly taken to be absolute. If each has a right to truth, we have to consider whether it "may be forfeited or suspended under certain circumstances" (ME 315). Sidgwick thinks the right might be forfeited in some cases. If we may kill in self-defence, because an attacker forfeits his right against being killed, it seems we may lie in self-defence, because someone threatening our rights forfeits his right to the truth. The conditions permitting killing in self-defence will certainly permit lying in self-defence, since lying is much less serious, morally speaking, than killing.

Sidgwick goes on to recount other cases in which common sense seems to grant the permissibility of lying. A lawyer is not always required to be truthful in defence of her client. She might within strict limits lie on her client's behalf if asked to do so. The advocate of common sense seems to permit benevolent lies, for example, lies told to invalids in cases where this is the only way to suppress facts that might produce a "dangerous shock" or to (young) children when we think they are better off not knowing the truth (ME 316). He further argues that if we admit benevolent lies, it is hard to

> see how we can decide when and how far it is admissible, except by considerations of expediency. (ME 316)

This suggests that the duty of veracity is not basic but rests ultimately on some other principle. One candidate principle, Sidgwick suggests, is utilitarian in nature.

There are further difficulties concerning the exact content of the common-sense obligation of veracity. Is it an obligation to:

1. ensure only that (as far as we can) our actual affirmations correspond to (what we believe to be) the truth or
2. ensure only (as far as we can) that the inferences that we foresee are likely to be drawn from what we say correspond to (what we believe to be) the truth.

Sidgwick describes how 1 and 2 come apart in cases where the truth is inferable only from "fictitious premises" (ME 317). If 2 makes up the obligation, we may tell a falsehood to discharge it. The obligation is to make sure the inferences drawn from what you say correspond to the truth, but since producing this may require making affirmations not corresponding to the truth, it is permissible to make such affirmations. In order to get people to believe that the right ratio between rest and labour is 1 : 6, it might be acceptable, Sidgwick remarks, to affirm the false belief that since God created the world in six days and rested on the seventh, 1 : 6 is the "divinely ordered proportion between rest and labour" (ME 316n2).

If 1 constitutes the obligation, we need only to ensure that our affirmations correspond to the truth. Veracity does not, in this case, include the obligation to ensure that the inferences drawn from our sincere avowals mirror (what we believe to be) the truth. This account of the obligation might be the right one for our world where

> concealment is frequently necessary to the well-being of society, and may be legitimately effected by any means short of actual falsehood. (ME 317)

Consider an example to illustrate. I have agreed with Melanie that she will care for my children every Tuesday after school. I meet William and think he will be better at caring. I want therefore to let Melanie go. I tell her my schedule has changed and I no longer wish to have her services. Both claims, let's suppose, are true, but it is untrue that the schedule change is the cause of my no longer wishing to have Melanie's services. But I foresee that when I tell her these things, she will infer that I do not need her because my schedule has changed. This belief is false.

According to 2, I don't discharge my obligation of veracity. I knowingly leave Melanie with a false belief that she has inferred from what I said. But on 1 I do discharge my obligation. Sticking to making sure that my statements correspond to the truth seems warranted by, say, the need not to hurt her feelings. Sidgwick says common sense is tempted by both views but gives no sense of which is right.

Why this is a problem for common-sense morality is not obvious. Might there be two obligations of veracity? Sidgwick will no doubt say if this is true, common sense will have to address (as it may have to in the case of promise-keeping) the "degrees of obligatoriness in duties" and it provides little clarity on this.[12]

He concludes that reflection seems to show that the obligation of veracity cannot be "elevated into a definite moral axiom" (ME 317):

> for there is no real agreement as to how far we are bound to impart true beliefs
> to others: and while it is contrary to Common Sense to exact candour under all
> circumstances, we yet find no self-evident secondary principle, clearly defin-
> ing when it is not to be exacted. (ME 317)

---

[12] Deontologists are themselves in disagreement about how to balance these two obligations; see, e.g., Broad, 1930: 219; Ross, 1939: 81–2.

Sidgwick's analysis of the common-sense obligation of veracity does not conclude here. He considers the possibility that the above exceptions and qualifications are "only admitted by Common Sense from inadvertence and shallowness of thought" (ME 317). The considered view of common sense might be that the requirement to tell the truth is absolute because were it "generally understood" lying is permitted in "certain circumstances,"

> it would immediately become quite useless to tell the lies, because no one would believe them. (ME 318)

A rule permitting lies would be suicidal and a moralist cannot lay down this kind of rule. Call this the self-defeat argument against lying. The conclusion is that lying is not permitted. Somewhat oddly, Sidgwick does not mention Kant here even though the position considered is clearly Kant's.[13]

Sidgwick does not say why he considers Kant's view. He raises several criticisms of it. But he need not have bothered. First, it seems clear that Kant's view does not represent common-sense morality. It is hard to deny, for example, the common-sense view that it is permissible to lie in cases where lying is a necessary means to defending oneself against a "palpable invasion of our rights" (ME 315).

Second, in a moment of moderation, Kant concedes it is permissible to lie in some cases because "if, in all cases, we were to remain faithful to every detail of the truth, we might often expose ourselves to the wickedness of others, who wanted to abuse our truthfulness" (Kant, 1997a: 27 :448). He goes on to say

> it is true that we often court danger by punctilious observance of the truth, and hence has arisen the concept of the necessary lie, which is a very critical point for the moral philosopher. For seeing that one may steal, kill or cheat from necessity, the case of emergency subverts the whole of morality, since if that is the plea, it rests upon everyone to judge whether he deems it an emergency or not; and since the ground here is not determined, as to where the emergency arises, the moral rules are not certain. For example, somebody, who knows that I have money, asks me: Do you have money at home? If I keep silent, the other concludes that I do. If I say yes, he takes it away from me; if I say no, I tell a lie; so what am I to do? So far as I am constrained, by force used against me, to make an admission, and a wrongful use is made of my statement, and I am unable to save myself by silence, the lie is a weapon of defence; the declaration extorted, that is then misused, permits me to defend myself, for whether my admission or my money is extracted, is all the same. Hence there is no case in which a necessary lie should occur, save where the declaration is wrung from me, and I am also convinced that the other means to make a wrongful use of it. (Kant, 1997a: 27:448)

---

[13] For the same point, see Crisp, 2015: 180. Kant gives something like this argument in Kant 2002: 4:402–3, 4:422.

In defending this view, Kant expresses sympathy with at least some of Sidgwick's objections to the absolutist position on lying (ME 318–19). Kant seems to concede Sidgwick's point that at least in some cases the erosion of mutual confidence produced by lying is beneficial, including where it prevents "rogues" benefitting from the "veracity of honest men" (ME 318).

Of course, Kant's more moderate position is less liberal than common-sense morality (as Sidgwick represents it) in respect of permissible lying. He seems not to allow for benevolent lies of the sort Sidgwick notes common sense permits us to tell the ill and young children in some cases. Sidgwick might object that if wrongful use of the sort Kant discusses permits lying, why can't the prevention of a "dangerous shock" to the ill or the corruption of a child's character or well-being do so, too (at least when the declaration is wrung from you)? The claim that it is permissible to lie in the latter cases seems no less plausible than the claim that it is permissible to lie the former case.[14] In any event, in accepting permissible lies, Kant seems to join Sidgwick in rejecting the self-defeat argument.

Sidgwick has two goals in investigating common-sense morality, to clarify its requirements and to verify whether it includes any intuitive truths (or higher certainties). Thus far, we have examined the first aim of his investigation, looking at his treatment of the obligation of veracity. Let's turn now to his second aim.

Sidgwick's examination of the main obligations of common-sense morality is conducted to prepare the materials for assessing whether it includes any "clear and precise principles commanding universal acceptance" (ME 338).

The dogmatic intuitionist claims to know the basic obligations of common-sense morality directly or non-inferentially, not by appeal to reasoning or inference (ME 101, 211, 338). The obligations to keep our promises and to tell the truth are not, the dogmatic intuitionist insists, obligations following from some more basic moral principle.[15] They are non-derivative moral requirements.

Sidgwick aims to determine whether, among others, the principle that we ought to tell the truth is of the highest certainty (i.e., satisfies conditions 1–4 set out in Section 2). He seeks to establish if the certainty of this obligation vanishes or not under scrutiny. He begins his quest in the *Methods* Book III, ch. xi, where he asks: Can any of "the deliverances of common sense ... be classed as Intuitive Truths" (ME 343)? Sidgwick offers the following, negative verdict:

> Now if the account given of the Morality of Common Sense in the preceding chapters be in the main correct, it seems clear that, generally speaking, its maxims do not fulfil the conditions just laid down. So long as they are left in

---

[14] Kant may agree; see Kant, 1996: 6:431.

[15] Ditto the obligations of beneficence, justice, and purity.

the state of somewhat vague generalities, as we meet them in ordinary discourse, we are disposed to yield them unquestioning assent, and it may be fairly claimed that the assent is approximately universal – in the sense that any expression of dissent is eccentric and paradoxical. But as soon as we attempt to give them the definiteness which science requires, we find that we cannot do this without abandoning the universality of acceptance. We find, in some cases, that alternatives present themselves, between which it is necessary that we should decide; but between which we cannot pretend that Common Sense does decide, and which often seem equally or nearly equally plausible. In other cases the moral notion seems to resist all efforts to obtain from it a definite rule: in others it is found to comprehend elements which we have no means of reducing to a common standard, except by the application of the Utilitarian – or some similar – method. Even where we seem able to educe from Common Sense a more or less clear reply to the questions raised in the process of definition, the principle that results is qualified in so complicated a way that its self-evidence becomes dubious or vanishes altogether. And thus in each case what at first seemed like an intuition turns out to be either the mere expression of a vague impulse, needing regulation and limitation which it cannot itself supply, but which must be drawn from some other source: or a current opinion, the reasonableness of which has still to be shown by a reference to some other principle. (ME 342–3)

Sidgwick's verdict is that in some cases we can achieve clarity and precision (we can satisfy condition 1) but only at the expense of disagreement (or failing to satisfy condition 4). In still other cases, we seem on reflection not to have an intuition at all (we fail to satisfy condition 2). Let's turn now to see the argument exhibited in the case of our example of the duty of veracity.

How does the obligation of veracity fare when Sidgwick's four conditions are applied to it? He suggests there is no agreement as to the fundamental nature of the obligation. It is not clear

whether it is our actual affirmation as understood by the recipient which we are bound to make correspond to fact (as far as we can), or whatever inferences we foresee that he is likely to draw from this, or both. (ME 355)

We saw before that there seem to be two obligations of veracity and, Sidgwick suggests, "perfect" candour and sincerity require discharging both. However, it is unclear given the needs of social well-being and tact that we ought to aim at perfection in every case. So while we may seem to have here two clear principles, there is no agreement on how to rank them or reconcile conflicts between them. This suggests that the obligation does not satisfy test 4 above.

In addition, the obligation is qualified: common sense admits that it is okay to lie to children in some cases and to "madmen, or invalids ... or to enemies or robbers, or even to persons who ask questions which they have no right to ask"

(ME 355). Kant even seemed in places to agree that there are exceptions to the requirement to tell the truth. He seemed keen to argue that lying is permissible in cases where it is the only way to prevent rogues benefitting from honest men. These qualifications, Sidgwick surmises, suggest the obligation rests on some more basic principle. His idea then seems to be that there is, on reflection, no intuition; we have instead come to our view of the obligation of veracity based on a "rapid and half-conscious" process of reasoning (ME 211–12). This suggests that the obligation does not satisfy test 2 above.

Sidgwick concludes that this principle of common-sense morality lacks the "characteristic of a scientific axiom" (ME 360). The obligation of veracity is not thereby deprived of practical significance, however. The main part of the obligation is clear. The morality of common sense may, then, "still be perfectly adequate to give practical guidance to common people in common circumstances" (ME 361).

Sidgwick arrives at similar conclusions about all the major rules of common sense. He says, for example, that the common-sense requirement of promise-keeping is not clear and precise because it fails to tell us what to do in cases where keeping a promise is costly to the promiser or the promisee. He notes disagreement, in the case of justice, about the correct basis for the distribution of the means of happiness, whether we ought to distribute in accordance with desert or in addition with fitness to effectively use the means distributed. He concludes that in common sense he cannot find anything resembling an "independent" intuition (ME 346, 348), a self-evident proposition (ME 346, 347, 348), a "clear intuition" (ME 347), a "primary" intuition (ME 347), a "moral axiom" (ME 352, 356), an "absolute first principle" (ME 355), and so on. The main moral opinions of common-sense morality resist scientific determination (ME 360).

Sidgwick aims in Book III, ch. xi to determine if there are any intuitive truths in common sense. He appears to think that if the principles of common-sense morality are not intuitive truths, they are opinions or vague impulses (ME 338, 343; PC 565). They might be justified, but not by appeal to common sense itself. (He later says that the main principles of common sense require "rational justification of some kind" (ME 383; IE 34–5).)

Some of Sidgwick's critics complain that his argument against common-sense morality assumes its main principles are absolute and do not omit of exceptions (Broad, 1930: 218–23; Hurka, 2014a: 135). Sidgwick's characterizations of the view often suggest this assumption (e.g., ME 200; PC 464–5). In characterizing common-sense morality this way, the objector insists, Sidgwick overlooks the more moderate account of the main principles of common-sense morality according to which they express, following Ross, *prima facie* obligations or obligations admitting of exceptions (Ross, 1930: 19–20; Broad, 1930: 222).

Sidgwick sometimes seems at least aware of something like the Rossian view in his discussions of promise-keeping and veracity. In clarifying the duty of veracity, he notes the need to balance the two requirements of "perfect" candour (ME 317) and he is sensitive to "degrees of obligatoriness in duties" in the context of clarifying the obligation to keep promises (ME 305; PE 78). Sidgwick puzzles mostly over the practical clarity of the main principles of common-sense morality. Ross's claim that obligations are *prima facie* does not solve this problem.

Indeed, Ross's *prima facie* duties of promise-keeping, reparation, and gratitude are often poorly specified (Ross, 1930: 21–27). Ross did remarkably little to clarify what he considered to be the main duties of common-sense morality. His attempt to clarify the obligation of fidelity to promises, for example, does not meet Sidgwick's challenge. Ross often simply reported that in the case of this obligation one must rely on interpretation in determining whether, for example, we ought to keep promises to a promisee who is dead or incapable of benefitting from fulfilment of a promise. (Ross, 1939: 87ff.; for discussion, see Hurka, 2014a: 141–42; Skelton, 2022). Sidgwick thinks we need to venture beyond common-sense morality to deal with the practical infelicities in common sense. He moves in this direction in part because he thinks, with Aristotle, we study ethics "for the sake of Practice: and in practice we are concerned with particulars" (ME 215).

Of course, critics may choose to resist the need to venture further (Broad, 1930: 223). In balancing duties or determining their precise content we may, like Ross, appeal to judgement (Ross, 1930: 42; see also Broad, 1930: 222–23). This is one option.[16] Another option involves penetrating more deeply to find concrete answers to moral questions using another method. Sidgwick hints common sense often seems to appeal to utilitarian considerations when thinking about how to sort out its difficulties or deal with imprecision (e.g., ME 354, 355). He suggests utilitarianism provides support and succour to the common-sense duties of promise-keeping and veracity (ME 443–4, 448–9). Is this, then, the way forward?

In this section, we wrestled with Sidgwick's attempt to clarify one principle of common-sense morality and to determine whether it could satisfy Sidgwick's epistemic tests. In the next section, we shall examine whether it is possible to locate intuitive truths or higher certainties outside of common-sense morality.

---

[16] Sidgwick may have dismissed this option too quickly. Crisp notes (rightly) that Sidgwick "ignores the possibility of practical judgement in particular cases" (190; also viii–ix, 4, 104, 114, 145, 192–4, 224n42, 231).

4 The Case for Utilitarianism

Sidgwick is unable to discover any intuitive truths (or higher certainties) in common-sense morality. Might it be possible to find intuitive truths (or higher certainties) elsewhere? Sidgwick answers this question in Book III, ch. xiii. He says he finds several such truths, some of which support utilitarianism (and, as we shall see, some of which support egoism) and ultimately a method of ethics (though not one excluding judgement entirely (ME 477)).

We noted before that Sidgwick is an epistemic intuitionist. Sidgwick calls the version of intuitionism he endorses philosophical intuitionism, on which there are "one or more principles more absolutely and undeniably true and evident" (ME 102). It is the philosopher's job, he says, to

> enunciate, in full breadth and clearness, those primary intuitions of Reason, by the scientific application of which the common moral thought of mankind may be at once systematized and corrected. (ME 373–4)

Philosophical intuitions are relied on, he says, "to tell men what they ought to think, rather than what they do think" (ME 373). Many moralists, Sidgwick reminds us, have tried to find philosophical intuitions. But they often fail to find more than "sham-axioms" or principles that are substantially tautological (ME 374). He is not discouraged. He thinks he can locate

> certain absolute practical principles, the truth of which, when they are explicitly stated, is manifest; but they are of too abstract a nature, and too universal in their scope, to enable us to ascertain by immediate application of them what we ought to do in any particular case; particular duties have still to be determined by some other method. (ME 379)

Sidgwick claims to find a number of such absolute practical principles, detailed in what follows.

4.1 Sidgwick's Philosophical Intuitions: First Pass

In Book III, ch. i Sidgwick says there is an important "practical rule" we arrive at by reflecting on the notion of rightness, that

> [w]e cannot judge an action to be right for A and wrong for B, unless we can find in the natures or circumstances of the two some difference which we can regard as a reasonable ground for difference in their duties. (ME 209)

Sidgwick thinks this practical rule is an important protection

> against the danger that besets the conscience, of being warped and perverted by strong desire, so that we too easily think that we ought to do what we very much wish to do. (ME 209)

We may state, Sidgwick says, a corresponding claim about what ought to be done to (rather than by) different individuals. Sidgwick considers the golden rule that you ought to do unto others what you would have others do unto you. He thinks the golden rule is "imprecise": one might have others help with vice and so be willing to help others with vice. A more precise version qualifying as a philosophical intuition he states as follows:

> it cannot be right for A to treat B in a manner in which it would be wrong for B to treat A, merely on the ground that they are two different individuals, and without there being any difference between the natures or circumstances of the two which can be stated as a reasonable ground for difference of treatment. (ME 380)

Let's call this J. J is basically a principle of universality declaring that any difference in the moral treatment of two people must be grounded in a difference in the facts about their respective situations. J throws "a definite *onus probandi* on the man who applies to another a treatment of which he would complain if applied to himself" (ME 380). Sidgwick thinks J qualifies as an intuitive truth (ME 381; ME1 296). It involves denying, for example, that proper names and indexicals constitute reasonable grounds for difference of treatment. It cannot be right for me to lie to you but wrong for you to lie to me simply on the grounds that we are different individuals. The fact that A is you and B is me is not alone sufficient to ground difference of treatment (ME1 183n2).

A second philosophical intuition is found, Sidgwick says, by reflection on the notion of an individual's good or prudence. The maxim of prudence, he notes, is sometimes thought to state that one ought to promote one's own good (e.g., happiness). However, understanding the maxim as claiming one ought to aim at one's own good does not, he warns, "clearly avoid tautology," for we might interpret "good" as "what one ought to aim at" (ME 381).[17] We would, Sidgwick thinks, in this case be claiming that we ought to aim at what we ought to aim at. It is possible to avoid tautology, he insists, if the maxim of prudence is understood as claiming that one ought to aim at one's own good *on the whole*.

The claim that one ought to aim at one's own good on the whole involves, for Sidgwick, a commitment to "impartial concern for all parts of our conscious life" (ME 381; also 111, 124n1). Impartiality of this sort involves denying the direct (or intrinsic) relevance of temporal location to the value of (say) an episode of happiness. An episode of happiness occuring now is not (merely in virtue of its location in time) of greater value than an episode of happiness of the same quantity occuring later. More generally, the idea is that the good of any one

---

[17] For the claim that Sidgwick's initial principle is not in fact a tautology, see Schneewind, 1977: 293. The principle is that we ought to aim at what we ought to aim at *for oneself*, and this is not a tautology.

period or moment in a life is of no more importance (from the point of view of the life as a whole) than the good of any other, unless they differ in quantity. So prudence involves giving equal weight to equal quantities of good (e.g., happiness) no matter when in life (the prime of life or senescence) they occur.

Sidgwick is, however, quick to clarify that impartiality of this sort (i.e., temporal neutrality) is consistent with (a) in some cases giving some priority to experiencing a good (going to a concert) in the present over experiencing a good of similar quantity in the future because the former is more certain or likely to occur and (b) in some cases giving priority to experiencing something in the future (sampling an expensive wine) over experiencing something in the present because by deferring the experience we will benefit more "through an increase in our means or capacities of happiness" (ME 381).

He says following this "[a]ll that the principle affirms" is

> the mere difference of priority and posteriority in time is not a reasonable
> ground for having more regard to the consciousness of one moment that [sic]
> to that of another. (ME 381)

Let's call this T. T *appears* to be what Sidgwick classifies as an intuitive truth.

The "practical" form T takes is that a smaller present good is not to be preferred to a future greater good (putting aside issues of certainty). The most common version of the principle is "present *pleasure* or *happiness* is reasonably to be foregone with the view of obtaining greater pleasure or happiness hereafter" (ME 381; italics in original). But he insists the hedonistic application is not the only one available; the principle holds for other interpretations of one's good (e.g., a view on which one's good consists in the possession of knowledge, achievement, and friendship) and so it should be distinguished from hedonism. Quantity of good is the central concern: the goods of each moment in one's life possess equal value (from the point of view of the life as a whole) unless there is a greater quantity of good in one moment than in another.

A third and fourth philosophical intuition can be discovered by examination of the notion of the universal or aggregate good which involves the "comparison and integration of the goods of all individual human – or sentient – existences" (ME 382). The third philosophical intuition says

> the good of any one individual is of no more importance, from the point of
> view (if I may say so) of the Universe, than the good of any other; unless, that
> is, there are special grounds for believing that more good is likely to be
> realised in the one case than in the other. (ME 382)

Let's call this P. P claims that the value of a good (happiness) does not vary with changes merely in who possesses it but it does vary with changes to its quantity.

The idea is that from the point of view of no one in particular a difference in the quantity or amount of good that two individuals possess is a reason to deviate from assigning equal value to the good those individuals possess. A greater quantity of good is of greater value.

The fourth philosophical intuition says

> that as a rational being I am bound to aim at good generally, – so far as it is attainable by my efforts, – not merely at a particular part of it. (ME 382)

Let's call this B. B seems to involve the claim that, if rational, I ought to aim at the general or aggregate good (e.g., happiness) not, say, merely the good of my children or the good (or happiness) of those to whom I have attachments.

From the third and fourth philosophical intuitions Sidgwick draws what he calls a "necessary inference," which he labels the maxim of rational benevolence:

> each one is morally bound to regard the good of any other individual as much
> as his own, except in so far as he judges it to be less, when impartially viewed,
> or less certainly knowable or attainable by him. (ME 382)

Sidgwick is unclear on the precise content of this inference. He says in various places that it enjoins the promotion of general or universal good and qualifies as an intuitive truth (ME xxxv, 387, 388, 400, 418, 421, 498, 507; UG 31). For Sidgwick, it expresses a core element of utilitarianism: "the axiom of Rational Benevolence is, in my view, required as a rational basis for the Utilitarian system" (ME 387; also 388). Simplifying, it says we ought to aim at general good, not merely at particular goods, giving equal weight to equal quantities of good. Let's call this RB.[18]

Sidgwick says his appeal to philosophical intuitions furnishes utilitarianism:

> Utilitarianism is thus presented as the final form into which Intuitionism tends
> to pass, when the demand for really self-evident first principles is rigorously
> pressed. (ME 388; also PC 564)

His use of "tends" is intentional. He has not yet secured all he needs to justify utilitarianism. A complete transition to utilitarianism, he admits, requires (justifiably) interpreting the notion "good" referred to in P, B, and RB as "happiness" (ME 388). In the following chapter, Book III, ch. xiv, he argues that happiness (pleasure) is the sole ultimate good; at the conclusion of this argument, he says

---

[18] In various places, Sidgwick describes RB as an intuition (e.g., ME 388, 400, 421, and 462n1). Sidgwick presents it is an inference from P and B (ME 382), suggesting that it is not known directly or by reflecting on its content. However, if the interpretation presented in Section 2 of condition 3 for higher certainty is correct, it seems possible for a proposition to be both an intuition and supported by inference.

> I am finally led to the conclusion (which at the close of the last chapter
> seemed to be premature) that the Intuitional method rigorously applied yields
> as its final result the doctrine of pure Universalistic Hedonism, – which it is
> convenient to denote by the single word, Utilitarianism. (ME 406–7)

At first blush, then, Sidgwick, accepts five philosophical intuitions, one of
which, RB, is a derivation from two others, P and B. Sidgwick's appeal to
philosophical intuitions raises a number of issues. Let's examine three.

4.2 Sidgwick's Philosophical Intuitions: Second Pass

The first issue is that it is in fact not clear on further reflection which propositions
Sidgwick thinks qualify as philosophical intuitions. Interpreters appear to agree that
Sidgwick accepts J, P, B, and the deduction, RB (see, e.g., Broad, 1930: 223–7;
Schneewind, 1977: 296–7; Donagan, 1992: 126–7; Shaver, 1999: 61–2; Skelton,
2008: 187–8; Nakano-Okuno, 2011: 93–100; Phillips, 2011: 96–7; Hurka, 2014a:
144–5; de Lazari-Radek and Singer, 2014: 116–19; Crisp, 2015: 116–21; Schultz,
2017: 251).

Sidgwick is a hedonist and so holds that

> Happiness (pleasure) is the sole ultimate good (e.g., UG 35–6; ME 406; GSM
> 126–31; EP 38–9).[19]

Let's call this H. Skelton (2008: 191–3), Irwin (2009: 497), Nakano-Okuno (2011:
129–30), and Crisp (2015: 209) agree that H is among the propositions Sidgwick
classifies as philosophical intuitions. Shaver (1999: 61–2, 2014), Phillips (2011: 97,
102, 111n7), and de Lazari-Radek and Singer (2014: 146n46) disagree.

There are good reasons to hold that Sidgwick means to present H as
a philosophical intuition. First, when he defends hedonism against its most
formidable foe – the view that knowledge, beauty, virtue, and freedom have non-
instrumental value whether they produce pleasure or not – he appeals to "intuitive
judgement after due consideration" (ME 400; also GSM 127) or the "immediate
intuition of reflective persons" (UG 35).

Second, when he finishes defending hedonism, he admits to relying in his
arguments for it and for his philosophical intuitions generally on the "Intuitional
method rigorously applied" (ME 406).

Third, he explicitly characterizes his hedonistic principles as "intuitional,"
and as having an "intuitive character":

> there is a wider sense in which the term 'intuitional' might be legitimately
> applied to either Egoistic or Universalistic Hedonism; so far as either system
> lays down as a first principle – which if known at all must be intuitively

---

[19] Sidgwick treats the term "happiness" as "convertible" with the term "pleasure" (ME 92).

> known – that happiness is the only rational ultimate end of action. To this
> meaning I shall recur in the concluding chapters (xiii. and xiv.) of ... Book
> [III]; in which I shall discuss more fully the intuitive character of these
> hedonistic principles. (ME 201)

Phillips says H is not among Sidgwick's philosophical intuitions.[20] He
provides two reasons for his view.

First, H is not, he says, one of Sidgwick's philosophical intuitions because it
is not dealt with in the chapter in which Sidgwick defends the bulk of his
philosophical intuitions.[21] But, as we have seen, Sidgwick states clearly that he
relies on intuition in the chapter in which he defends H. He works through rivals
to hedonism, pointing out their infelicities in an effort to lead his readers to H in
much the same way he interrogates common-sense morality to lead his readers
to, for example, J, P, B, and RB.

Second, H is not among Sidgwick's philosophical intuitions because, Phillips
insists, Sidgwick concedes his argument for H is not "completely cogent" (ME
401). Sidgwick notes common sense resists hedonism: "several cultivated persons do habitually judge that knowledge, art, etc. – not to speak of Virtue – are
ends independently of the pleasure derived from them" (ME 401; also UG 35). He
is undeterred. As in the case of his other philosophical intuitions, when he
encounters disagreement he tries to find a way to minimize it (UG 35).

For example, he observes that the common-sense obligation of benevolence
falls short of his maxim of benevolence, or RB. According to common-sense
morality, benevolence, unlike RB, permits giving priority at the theoretical level
to the good or happiness of those to whom we have attachments or close
relations (ME 242, 252–3, 382). In reply, Sidgwick says that in practice RB
permits this kind of partiality. General happiness is promoted best when each of
us concerns herself

> with promoting the good of a limited number of human beings, and that generally
> in proportion to the closeness of their connection with ... [her]. (ME 382)

Another example of reconciliation occurs when Sidgwick confronts the suggestion
that according to common-sense morality knowledge, virtue, beauty, and freedom
are non-instrumentally good. He makes a move like the one above. He argues

> the pursuit of the ideal objects before mentioned, Virtue, Truth, Freedom,
> Beauty, etc., *for their own sakes*, is indirectly and secondarily, though not
> primarily and absolutely, rational; on account not only of the happiness that

---

[20] For another argument for the same position, see de Lazari-Radek and Singer, 2014: 146n46; for
a reply, see Skelton, 2019.

[21] Phillips himself locates a philosophical intuition outside this chapter, in the concluding chapter
of the *Methods* (Phillips, 2011: 129).

> will result from their attainment, but also of that which springs from their
> disinterested pursuit. While yet if we ask for a final criterion of the compara-
> tive value of the different objects of men's enthusiastic pursuit, and of the
> limits within which each may legitimately engross the attention of mankind,
> we shall none the less conceive it to depend upon the degree in which they
> respectively conduce to Happiness. (ME 405–6; italics in original)

Disagreement with "cultivated" people is not decisive evidence against including H among the propositions Sidgwick presents (or thinks qualify) as philosophical intuitions. He notes the disagreement and then deals with it in a way
that suggests that he thinks, as in the case of RB, the disagreement need not
reduce his confidence below that needed for affirming philosophical intuitions.

Continuing our investigation into which propositions Sidgwick thinks qualify
as philosophical intuitions, let us turn to T. In the context of his defence of T,
Sidgwick focuses on the notion of one's own good on the whole. T says mere
location in time is not alone directly (intrinsically) relevant to the value of
contributions to this whole. A number of interpreters maintain that Sidgwick
accepts T as self-evident and that in Book III, ch. xiii he means to defend only
T as one of his philosophical intuitions (Hayward, 1901: 122, 133–7; Broad,
1930: 225–6; Schneewind, 1977: 294, 296, 361; Donagan, 1992: 126–7;
Shaver, 1999: 74–7; Skelton, 2008: 200–01; Nakano-Okuno, 2011: 96–9,
104; Phillips, 2011: 96–7; Schultz, 2017: 251).

Other interpreters disagree (Irwin, 2009: 497; Hurka, 2014a: 144–5, 2014b:
158; Crisp, 2015: 117–19). Sidgwick endorses, on their view, something more
robust:

> One ought to aim at one's own good on the whole.

Let's call this O. There are good reasons for thinking Sidgwick embraces O and not
just T. Sidgwick is focused on one's good on the whole in his discussion of T and
the temporal neutrality it expresses. He is concerned to avoid putting forward
tautological intuitions or sham-axioms, for example, it is right to act rationally
(ME 374–9). In articulating an intuition relating to prudence, he is concerned to
brush this worry aside and offer a moral principle "of real significance" (ME 379).
This explains why his attention is focused on temporal neutrality. It is key, in his
view, to avoiding the tautology worry raised with respect to the maxim of prudence.
If the maxim is that one ought to aim at one's own good on the whole, not merely at
a particular part of it, giving equal weight to equal quantities of good regardless of
where in time they fall in one's life, it is not tautologous.

At the same time, he wants to ward off misunderstanding about what the
impartiality built into temporal neutrality involves (GSM 169–70). He is concerned to explain the permissibility of partiality to some particular part or

moment in a lifetime in a way similar to how he explains that RB permits some partiality toward particular individuals on grounds of special attachment (ME 382). In the case of prudence, he argues (as noted above) for the permissibility of partiality based on considerations of certainty and time's impact on expanding capacities for enjoyment. When Sidgwick says "[a]ll that the principle affirms" he should not be read as saying this is all the axiom affirms. He is saying all the claim about impartiality affirms is temporal neutrality, not, say, strict equality. He is not saying the axiom comprises only this. He is trying to defend the claim one ought to aim at one's own good generally, not merely at a particular part of it, while avoiding tautology. He does this through clarifying temporal neutrality as a central part of the philosophical intuition regarding prudence. The resulting intuition is that

> one ought to aim at own's good on the whole, not merely at a particular part of it, giving equal weight to equal quantities of good.

There are three reasons (which I shall now present but later rebut) against O being among Sidgwick's philosophical intuitions.

First, he claims at the conclusion of his articulation of the bulk of his philosophical intuitions that he has arrived at utilitarianism (ME 387, 388). He states this initially with some hesitancy. He admittedly still needs to establish hedonism, a salient component of utilitarianism. But once he finishes defending hedonism he says "the Intuitional method rigorously applied yields as its final result . . . Utilitarianism" (ME 406–7). This confidence is hard to reconcile with the acceptance of O as a *philosophical intuition*.

Second, the discussion in which Sidgwick putatively defends only T is present in the second and third edition of the *Methods* but Sidgwick says that in those editions he was guilty of failing to provide "sufficient rational justification, so far as Egoism is concerned" (FC 484). When he attempts to remedy this defect, he does not mention O. He appeals instead to the distinction between individuals:

> It would be contrary to Common Sense to deny that the distinction between any one individual and any other is real and fundamental, and that consequently "I" am concerned with the quality of my existence as an individual in a sense, fundamentally important, in which I am not concerned with the quality of the existence of other individuals: and this being so, I do not see how it can be proved that this distinction is not to be taken as fundamental in determining the ultimate end of rational action for an individual. (ME 498; also FC 484)

Third, Sidgwick says in the third and fourth editions of the *Methods* that egoism is "based" on the maxim of prudence (ME3 388; ME4 386–7). Starting in the fifth edition the language is altered; he says instead it is "implied in" rational egoism (ME5 387; ME 386). But O is not merely implied in rational egoism

(Shaver, 1999: 76); it may be relied on to provide support for rational egoism, the view that one ought to aim *only* at one's own happiness on the whole, not merely at a particular part of it, giving equal weight to equal quantities of happiness.

These reasons are inconclusive. Replies to them will be given in reverse order.

One might reply to the third reason by pointing out the oddity of suggesting a close connection between the maxim of prudence and rational egoism if the maxim expresses only T. T is, after all, implied in utilitarianism and other views, as is J (ME 387, 380). Noting a close connection between egoism and the maxim of prudence is more natural if the maxim of prudence is O. Sidgwick admits at times even in later editions that the maxim of prudence is the "logical basis" of egoism as RB is the logical basis of utilitarianism (ME 517). Sidgwick was perhaps misleading or not attempting to convey anything important in altering the language from "based" on to "implied in." Retaining the language of ME's earlier editions fits with Sidgwick's remarks about the content of the maxim of prudence, according to which it is a precept to seek

> one's own good on the whole, repressing all seductive impulses prompting to undue preference of particular goods. (ME 391–2; also 7, 119–20, 255, 386, 418, 498, 508; FC 483)

It is plausible that O implies rational egoism when held in conjunction with other claims. Shaver says O "virtually" implies egoism (Shaver, 1999: 76). This is too strong. O implies rational egoism presumably in the same way P and B (and RB) imply utilitarianism (i.e., only when defended in conjunction with other views one defends, including, in the case of egoism, hedonism, the absence of non-egoistic reasons, and the distinction between individuals, among others).

In reply to the second reason, it is important to emphasise Sidgwick's claim that he failed in earlier editions to supply "sufficient rational justification" for rational egoism. This is consistent with having supplied some justification for the view. O provides some, but perhaps not sufficient, justification for egoism. O is a claim about what we ought to do other things equal rather than all things considered. To provide sufficient justification for rational egoism one would need to defend not only hedonism, the absence of non-egoistic reasons, and so on, but crucially the *assumptions* of its key supports, for example, the distinction between individuals, which is an assumption of O (FC 484). Sidgwick, it seems, focusses on the distinction between individuals because he did not previously defend this assumption of O and of rational egoism. This is a very compelling way of conceiving of the role of the distinction between individuals in Sidgwick's argument for rational egoism (since thinking of it as playing a greater role than this in justifying rational egoism is not plausible, as we shall see).[22]

In order to reply to the first reason, it helps to revisit Sidgwick's epistemic conditions described in Section 2. Condition 4 calls for the absence of expert dissensus. If Sidgwick is serious about this condition, he cannot on reflection maintain that P, B, and RB alone secure utilitarianism. After outlining these philosophical intuitions, he confesses he should

> rely less confidently on the conclusions set forth in the preceding section, if they did not appear to me to be in substantial agreement – in spite of superficial differences – with the doctrines of those moralists who have been most in earnest in seeking among commonly received moral rules for genuine intuitions of the Practical Reason. (ME 384)

He thinks Kant and Clarke concur with J and RB (ME 384–6). If true, Sidgwick cannot think RB enjoins that we ought, morally, to aim only at universal or aggregate good. Neither Kant nor Clarke agrees to this. He must think it claims more modestly that one ought to aim at general good, not merely a particular part of it, giving equal weight to equal quantities of good, leaving open the possibility that other principles might compete with it, including O, which, like RB, looks like an *other things equal* principle rather than an *all things considered* principle. Only this version of RB has a chance of skirting expert dissensus.

Sidgwick claims, we noted, that utilitarianism is the view into "which Intuitionism tends to pass" (ME 388). This might be hard to square with the endorsement of O. He uses "tends" officially because he has yet to secure hedonism. But there may be other explanations for why he holds that his argument (at this stage) only *tends* in utilitarianism's direction.

One explanation is that he thinks utilitarians agree with O and that since his philosophical intuitions state other things equal principles rather than all things considered principles (Shaver, 2014: 184–93), he has more work to do to establish utilitarianism beyond establishing hedonism. It is not clear, however, that utilitarians can agree to O as a philosophical intuition. Utilitarians might agree that one ought to aim at one's own good on the whole, but only because one ought to aim at general good of which one's good on the whole forms a part. But as Sidgwick suggests, O is, contrary to utilitarianism, an obligation "independently of one's relation to" others (ME 386).

Another, better explanation is that he accepts O in addition to P, B, and RB. He sees that Butler, Clarke, Kant, and Mill agree with RB. He also sees that Butler, Clarke (though only indirectly (ME 120, 384n4)), and perhaps Plato and Aristotle

---

²² For discussion of the distinction passage and its role in establishing egoism, see Shaver, 1999: 82–98; 2020. More on this in the next section.

(whose influence on Sidgwick's "treatment of this subject has been greater than that of any modern writer" (ME 375n1) agree with O (ME 91–2), but that his two masters – Kant and Mill – reject O (ME 36, 366, 386, xx). He might think at this point RB has a slight edge over O, given that more of those competent to judge favour RB than O. He may think at this stage that it is rational to have more confidence in RB than in O. So while he cannot establish utilitarianism, he might be able to say that he has greater confidence that things are moving or tending in that direction.[23]

On second pass, then, it seems reasonable to interpret Sidgwick as embracing six philosophical intuitions: J, O, P, B, RB, and H. These are, again:

> J: it cannot be right for A to treat B in a manner in which it would be wrong for B to treat A, merely on the ground that they are two different individuals, and without there being any difference between the natures or circumstances of the two which can be stated as a reasonable ground for difference of treatment. (ME 380)

> O: one ought to aim at own's good on the whole, not merely at a particular part of it, giving equal weight to equal quantities of good (ME 381; also 391–2, 418, 498; FC 483).

> P: the good of any one individual is of no more importance, from the point of view (if I may say so) of the Universe, than the good of any other; unless, that is, there are special grounds for believing that more good is likely to be realised in the one case than in the other. (ME 382)

> B: that as a rational being I am bound to aim at good generally, – so far as it is attainable by my efforts, – not merely at a particular part of it. (ME 382)

> RB: we ought to aim at general good, not merely at a particular part of it, giving equal weight to equal quantities of good. (ME 382)

> H: Happiness (pleasure) is the sole ultimate good (e.g., UG 35–6; ME 406; GSM 126–31; EP 38–9).

4.3 Sidgwick's Philosophical Intuitions: Their Strength and Role

Let's turn now to investigate the second issue relating to Sidgwick's reliance on philosophical intuitions, which focusses on the strength of the philosophical intuitions and what one may conclude from them. Sidgwick's claim to have arrived at utilitarianism, we noted above, cannot be maintained if he hopes to show that his philosophical intuitions satisfy condition 4 described in Section 2,

---

[23] He also might put more emphasis on the philosophical intuitions supporting utilitarianism than on those supporting rational egoism because the "*onus probandi* lies with those who maintain that disinterested conduct, as such, is reasonable" (ME 120).

for, as we noted, the way to satisfy this condition is to argue that the intuitions state *other things equal* rather than *all things considered* principles. There are good reasons for thinking this is Sidgwick's considered view.

First, he says at one point in Book III, ch. xiii that he has secured the first principle of utilitarianism rather than utilitarianism itself:

> I find that I arrive, in my search for really clear and certain ethical intuitions, at the fundamental principle of Utilitarianism. I must, however, admit that the thinkers who in recent times have taught this latter system, have not, for the most part, expressly tried to exhibit the truth of their first principle by means of any such procedure as that above given. (ME 387)

He suggests the first principle is that we ought to promote good generally, not merely a particular part of it, giving equal weight to equal quantities of good regardless of who possesses it. At the outset of Book III, ch. xiv he says at this point in the argument he has established the principle that one ought to seek "others' good no less than one's own, repressing any undue preference for one individual over another" (ME 392). He does not see this as ruling out other principles, including O, which he mentions in the same place.

Second, in his discussion of hedonism he maintains it is no less "reasonable for an individual to take his own happiness as his ultimate end" than it is to take the general happiness as his ultimate end (ME 404n1). He could not say this were he really advocating for utilitarianism on the basis of the philosophical intuitions alone.

Finally, in Book IV, ch. ii when referring to the discussion of Book III, ch. xiii he says

> the reasoning that I used in chap. xiii. of the preceding book in exhibiting the principle of Rational Benevolence as one of the few Intuitions which stand the test of rigorous criticism ... as addressed to the [Dogmatic] Intuitionist ... only shows the Utilitarian first principle to be *one* moral axiom: it does not prove that it is *sole* or *supreme*. (ME 421; italics in original)

If Sidgwick's appeal to philosophical intuitions establishes only the first principle of utilitarianism, then the "final result" that the "Intuitional method rigorously applied yields" must be no more than the maxim of rational benevolence, a claim about what we ought to do other things equal.

At the conclusion, then, of Book III is a set of philosophical intuitions (J, O, P, B, RB, and H). To clarify Sidgwick's argument for utilitarianism we shall pay attention to the intuitions most relevant to it.[24] From P and B Sidgwick gets RB or

---

[24] We shall defer discussion of the philosophical intuitions relevant to rational egoism to the next section.

> each one is morally bound to regard the good of any other individual as much
> as his own, except in so far as he judges it to be less, when impartially viewed,
> or less certainly knowable or attainable by him. (ME 382)

RB amounts to the claim that we ought to advance general good, giving equal weight to equal quantities of good, regardless of who possesses it. Together with H

> Happiness (pleasure) is the sole ultimate good (e.g., ME 406; UG 35–6; GSM 126–31)

we get

> each one is morally bound to regard the happiness of any other individual as
> much as his own, except in so far as he judges it to be less, when impartially
> viewed, or less certainly knowable or attainable by him.

Or, more simply, we ought to promote general happiness, giving equal weight to equal quantities of happiness, regardless of who possesses it. Let us call this HRB. At the conclusion of Book III, Sidgwick is, then, part way to utilitarianism. He must establish a number of utilitarianism's other elements before he is able to conclude in its favour.

One key element of utilitarianism (and egoism) is maximization. Sidgwick's utilitarianism is committed to the maximization of the greatest happiness (ME 411), by which he means "the greatest possible surplus of pleasure over pain" (ME 413). Maximization is not obviously part of HRB unless regarding the good of another as much as one's own involves maximization, which is likely Sidgwick's (unargued for) view. It is to him anyway obvious that we ought to maximize the good in the case of egoism (ME 381) and more generally (GSM 110).[25]

We might then interpret HRB as amounting to the claim we ought to maximize general or aggregate happiness. Securing utilitarianism requires Sidgwick to convince us that HRB is the only basic moral requirement. Establishing HRB's supremacy involves, for Sidgwick, showing, first, that common-sense morality includes only subordinate and dependent principles, second, that HRB satisfies Sidgwick's epistemic conditions, and, third, that utilitarianism supports, clarifies, and systematizes common-sense moral decision making.

The first two elements of this argument seem to show that HRB is supreme and the third element functions to move common-sense morality to fully embrace that result. Sidgwick describes this last component as involving

---

[25] Sidgwick thinks utilitarianism must be supplemented by a principle of equality to deal with cases in which the outcomes of one's options have the same quantity of happiness but where in one option the happiness is more equitably distributed than in the other option (ME 416–17). For discussion, see Irwin, 2009: 513–16; Shaver, 2014; Skelton, 2019.

> a line of argument which on the one hand allows the validity, to a certain extent, of the maxims already accepted, and on the other hand shows them to be not absolutely valid, but needing to be controlled and completed by some more comprehensive principle. (ME 420)

Sidgwick grants common-sense morality some kind of validity and upon this tries to usher common sense to utilitarianism. Sidgwick is relying on a form of proof he adopts from Mill which involves providing the common-sense moralist with (rational) considerations determining her mind to accept utilitarianism.[26] This involves showing

> how Utilitarianism sustains the general validity of the current moral judgments, and thus supplements the defects which reflection finds in the intuitive recognition of their stringency; and at the same time affords a principle of synthesis, and a method for binding the unconnected and occasionally conflicting principles of common moral reasoning into a complete and harmonious system. If systematic reflection upon the morality of Common Sense thus exhibits the Utilitarian principle as that to which Common Sense naturally appeals for that further development of its system which this same reflection shows to be necessary, the proof of Utilitarianism seems as complete as it can be made. (ME 422; also UG 31–2)

Sidgwick thinks this completes the argument for utilitarianism as against the common-sense moralist. It involves showing, first, that there are no intuitive truths in common-sense morality, second, that there exist intuitive truths supporting utilitarianism and, third, that utilitarian has the capacity to support and clarify the main principles of common-sense morality, including the principle of veracity (ME 448–9). We shall return to this argument below.

4.4 Sidgwick's Appeal to Philosophical Intuitions: Some Problems

We can now examine the final issue related to Sidgwick's appeal to philosophical intuitions in his argument for utilitarianism. It targets the first two elements of it. The charge is that he is unfair to the dogmatic intuitionist because he treats the philosophical intuitions he accepts much less harshly than he treats the intuitions of common-sense morality.[27]

Sidgwick thinks the philosophical intuitions he offers constitute

---

[26] The debate over the precise nature of this proof is vexed. Some think it involves attributing probative value to common-sense morality and arguing that utilitarianism receives support by capturing and explaining the main elements of common-sense morality; others think it is an *ad hominem* argument against common-sense morality. For discussion, see Singer, 1974; Sverdlik, 1985; Brink, 1994; Shaver, 1999: 62–74; Skelton, 2010; Hurka, 2014b: 120–01; Crisp, 2015: 105–7, 211.

[27] For this charge, see Skelton, 2008; Phillips, 2011: 100–03; Hurka, 2014a, 2014b: 158–64.

> certain absolute practical principles, the truth of which, when they are
> explicitly stated, is manifest; but they are of too abstract a nature, and too
> universal in their scope, to enable us to ascertain by immediate application of
> them what we ought to do in any particular case; particular duties have still to
> be determined by some other method. (ME 379)

Sidgwick's first epistemic condition, recall, requires intuitions to render clear and precise practical guides. He dismisses common-sense intuitions in part because they fail on this score. By contrast, he does not insist on such clarity and precision from his own intuitions. He does not require his philosophical intuitions to tell us what to do in particular situations. He requires the intuitions of common-sense morality to satisfy a demand he does not apply to his own intuitions. Sidgwick is therefore unfair.

This is a powerful objection. How might it be deflected, if at all?

Sidgwick might try to blunt the force of the objection by pointing out that common sense agrees with some of his intuitions, including (perhaps) O and RB. He remarks

> No Intuitionist ever maintained that *all* our conduct can be ordered rightly
> without any calculation of its effects on human happiness. On the contrary,
> this calculation, for ourselves and for others, is expressly inculcated by the
> maxims of Prudence and Benevolence, as commonly understood. (PC 564;
> italics in original; also GSM 331–2)

The problems Sidgwick's intuitions face will, then, be ones those agreeing to them will have to contend with, too. Anyone embracing HRB will have to decide on whether to advance average or total happiness as Sidgwick does, for example (ME 415–16), or to advocate for maximizing over satisficing. The worries are not uniquely Sidgwick's. Replying in this way is dangerous, however: it might force us to conclude that there are no intuitions of any kind satisfying Sidgwick's conditions.

No doubt Sidgwick will urge against this, considering it would be

> disheartening to have to regard as altogether illusory the strong instinct of
> Common Sense that points to the existence of such principles, and the
> deliberate convictions of the long line of moralists who have enunciated
> them. (ME 379)

The cost of sticking with this instinct is, he might argue, that we shall find only principles of the sort his argument tries to sway us to accept, which are "not sufficient by themselves to give complete practical guidance" (ME xxxv).

This might be true, but nothing about this claim indicates the superiority of Sidgwick's intuitions over the intuitions found in common-sense morality. After all, he concedes the main principles of common-sense morality offer adequate practical guidance to "common people in common circumstances" (ME 361). Sidgwick's philosophical intuitions seem to fare no better than at least some of those in common sense that he patiently interrogates and discards.

The best that Sidgwick might do here is suggest that while philosophical intuitions cannot themselves determine our particular duties, they (unlike common-sense morality) point to a method that does. When Sidgwick suggests that particular duties have to be determined by some other method, his point must be such duties will have to be determined by some method other than the a priori dogmatic intuitionist method. The only other (useable) method is adopted by utilitarian and egoistic positions, which his intuitions urge us toward.

Interpreting Sidgwick this way fits with his claim that appeal to philosophical intuitions will not reveal "any definite code of absolute rules, applicable to all human beings without exception" (ME 379). The absence of a revealed code is implied, it seems, by Sidgwick's understanding of what the first principle of utilitarianism supplies:

> the acceptance of this principle gets us very little way towards a system of legislation: since we find it admitted equally by persons differing profoundly in their political aims and tendencies ... Hence, when we have agreed to take general happiness as the ultimate end, the most important part of our work still remains to be done: we have to establish or assume some subordinate principle or principles, capable of more precise application, relating to the best means for attaining by legislation the end of Maximum Happiness. (EP 40)

This reply will not suffice. First, Sidgwick must concede that his intuitions themselves fail condition 1 of his epistemic conditions which calls for clear and precise guidance in practice. His intuitions do not themselves provide complete practical guidance. Sidgwick might wish in this case to deny that the clarity and precision condition requires clarity and precision in practical guidance. But this denial would be costly. Sidgwick will have to find a fault with common-sense morality other than lack of practical clarity and precision and this fault will have to be specific to common-sense morality.

Second, Sidgwick concedes the method associated with utilitarianism does not in every case reveal clear and precise practical guidance. He catalogues the difficulties plaguing our ability to secure precision in quantitative comparisons between pleasures and pains (ME 132ff.). He thinks in the case of both egoism and utilitarianism that these difficulties significantly impair the practicality of the method they involve (ME 150, 289, 413–14, 460, 477; UG 38). By his own criteria, he ought to reject it.

It might suffice to cling to the empirical method if its problems seem more soluble than those allegedly facing common-sense morality. Unfortunately,

Sidgwick merely assumes that there is no option other than the empirical method (ME 150, 477). Perhaps he thinks we are more likely to improve the empirical method than the a priori method of dogmatic intuitionism (ME 101; GSM 106–07). But it is difficult to determine if the empirical method is more likely to be improved or if it is more likely, how much more likely. The common-sense moralist might side with Parfit and say because ethics is in its infancy it is not irrational to have high hopes for improvement in its own method (Parfit, 1984: 454).

The best Sidgwick can do to show the superiority of his principle is find some other way to diminish common-sense morality without at the same time diminishing his own. In various places he offers an argument based on reflection against the existence of independent truths in common-sense morality.

> I regard the apprehension, with more or less distinctness, of these abstract truths, as the permanent basis of the common conviction that the fundamental precepts of morality are essentially reasonable. No doubt these principles are often placed side by side with other precepts to which custom and general consent have given a merely illusory air of self-evidence: but the distinction between the two kinds of maxims appears to me to become manifest by merely reflecting upon them. I know by direct reflection that the propositions, 'I ought to speak the truth,' 'I ought to keep my promises' – however true they may be – are not self-evident to me; they present themselves as propositions requiring rational justification of some kind. On the other hand, the propositions, 'I ought not to prefer a present lesser good to a future greater good,' and 'I ought not to prefer my own lesser good to the greater good of another,' do present themselves as self-evident; as much (e.g.) as the mathematical axiom that 'if equals be added to equals the wholes are equal.' (ME 383)

> the principle that another's greater good is to be preferred to one's own lesser good is, in my view, the fundamental principle of morality – the ultimate, irreducible basis to which reflection shows the commonly accepted rules of Veracity, Good Faith, &c., to be subordinate. (FC 483)

> If I ask myself whether I see clearly and distinctly the self-evidence of any particular maxims of duty, as I see that of the formal principles "that what is right for me must be right for all persons in precisely similar circumstances" and "that I ought to prefer the greater good of another to my own lesser good:" I have no doubt whatever that I do not. I am conscious of a strong impression, an opinion on which I habitually act without hesitation, that I ought to speak truth, to perform promises, to requite benefits, &c., and also of powerful moral sentiments prompting me to the observance of these rules; but on reflection I can now clearly distinguish such opinions and sentiments from the apparently immediate and certain cognition that I have of the formal principles above mentioned. (PC 565)

Unfortunately, this strategy is weak. Sidgwick's hope is that his critical examination of common-sense morality will leave his reader's views "importantly modified" (PC 565). What he hopes is that after grasping the way in which, for example, the principles of promise-keeping and veracity need to be qualified, one will see the main rules of common-sense morality as subordinate and dependent and needing to be clarified and completed by a more basic principle like utilitarianism or egoism.

However, this is not the only way in which his reader's views might be importantly modified. The dogmatic intuitionist might modify her view to recognize a plurality of principles having a status much like Sidgwick's philosophical intuitions. Sidgwick permits the existence of a plurality of *other things equal* principles, including O and RB. One might ask why allow O and RB when you do not allow for the possibility of two duties of veracity needing to be balanced against one another? Sidgwick admits that the duties of veracity and promise-keeping may be "perfectly adequate to give practical guidance to common people in common circumstances" (ME 361) and as such appear no worse than his own principles.

This reflection argument against common-sense morality is a dangerous one for Sidgwick to offer. One might come on reflection to see O or RB as themselves subordinate and dependent. Sidgwick is aware of this threat. He notes that Kant thinks something like HRB may be derivative (ME 386). Sidgwick goes to great lengths to rebuff Kant's proposal (ME 389–90). Kant's position on the subordinate and derivate status of prudence is, of course, well-known (as we shall discover in the next section) (ME 36, 366).

Putting this aside, even if Sidgwick can limit the damage associated with the unfairness argument, he most certainly will find it hard to show that all the propositions he puts forward as philosophical intuitions pass test 4 of his tests for highest certainty. We before noted that Sidgwick presents H as a philosophical intuition. Was he right to do so? H is rejected by many seemingly no more likely to be in error than Sidgwick. Sidgwick thinks all pleasures are non-instrumentally good. However, some pleasures, it is widely held, are bad, including undeserved pleasures, pleasures taken in cruelty, pleasures taken in lust, and pleasures taken in the undeserved misfortune of others.

Kant writes

> that total well-being and contentment with one's condition that we call *'happiness'*, can make a person bold but consequently often reckless as well, unless a good will is present to correct their influence on the mind, thus adjusting the whole principle of one's action to render it conformable to universal ends. It goes without saying that the sight of a creature enjoying uninterrupted prosperity, but never feeling the slightest pull of a pure and good will, cannot excite approval in a rational and impartial spectator. Consequently, a good will seems to constitute the indispensable condition even of our worthiness to be happy. (Kant, 2002: 4:393; italics in original)

Hastings Rashdall writes

> return to our bull-fight, upon any rational or intelligible view of the compara-
> tive values of pleasure and pain, the intense pleasure which such spectacles
> give to thousands of beholders must surely outweigh the pain inflicted on
> a few dozen animals or even a few dozen criminals. If ten thousand spectators
> would not be sufficient to readjust the balance, suppose them multiplied
> tenfold or one-hundredfold. A humane man would condemn the spectacle
> all the same. He will pronounce such pleasures of inhumanity bad, quite apart
> from the somewhat dubious calculation that the encouragement of inhuman-
> ity in one direction tends to callousness in another. (Rashdall, 1924: 98–9)

G. E. Moore writes

> It is commonly held that certain of what would be called the lowest forms of
> sexual enjoyment, for instance, are positively bad, although it is by no means
> clear that they are not the most pleasant states we ever experience. Common
> Sense would certainly not think it a sufficient justification for the pursuit of what
> Prof. Sidgwick calls the 'refined pleasures' here and now, that they are the best
> means to the future attainment of a heaven, in which there would be no more
> refined pleasures–no contemplation of beauty, no personal affections–but in
> which the greatest possible pleasure would be obtained by a perpetual indulgence
> in bestiality. (Moore, 1903: 95)

Ross writes

> We have a decided conviction that there are bad pleasures . . . We think that the
> pleasure taken either by the agent or by a spectator in, for instance, a lustful or
> cruel action is bad; and we think it a good thing that people should be pained
> rather than pleased by contemplating vice or misery. (Ross, 1930: 136–7)

C. D. Broad writes

> Now consider the state of mind which is called "malice". Suppose that I perceive or
> think of the undeserved misfortunes of another man with pleasure. Is it not
> perfectly plain that this is an intrinsically bad state of mind, not merely *in spite
> of*, but *because of*, its pleasantness? Is it not plain that any cognition which has the
> relational property of being a cognition of another's undeserved misfortunes and
> the hedonic quality of pleasantness will be *worse* in proportion as the pleasantness
> is more intense? (Broad, 1930: 234; italics in original; for Sidgwick's discussion of
> malice, see IE, 40–1; ME 202–3)

Competent judges (or so we might assume) disagree with Sidgwick; H seems to
fail condition 4 of Sidgwick's epistemic tests. If Sidgwick is forced to give up
hedonism, his argument for utilitarianism may be vulnerable on two fronts. First,
his intuitions may be impugned for lacking clarity and precision because they
refer only to the good rather than to a specific good. He faults non-hedonistic

egoistic views for not providing definite accounts of the good (ME 91–2). Second, without hedonism Sidgwick will be unable to systematize common-sense morality fully in the way he proposes. He will be left to rely on judgement like his dogmatic intuitionist foe (M 569).

Sidgwick might be able to deflect some of these worries.[28] This would not put him in the clear; he has still to contend with the rational egoist, who rejects RB.

This might be too quick. On one interpretation, rational egoists may agree to P, B, and RB if the phrase "from the point of view of the universe" is affixed to the beginning of each philosophical intuition (Nakano-Okuno, 2011: 100, 105, 151–2; Shaver, 2014: 176–84). B and RB would, for example, take the following form:

> from the point of view of the universe I ought to "aim at good generally, – so far as it is attainable by my efforts, – not merely at a particular part of it" (ME 382).

> from the point of view of the universe "each one is morally bound to regard the good of any other individual as much as his own, except in so far as he judges it to be less, when impartially viewed, or less certainly knowable or attainable by him" (ME 382).

P, B, and RB state what is true from the point of view of the universe. Egoists might agree with what is true from this point of view, but at the same time resist taking up this point of view. What is true from the point of view of the universe has no practical implications for them.

Two reasons exist for rejecting this interpretation. First, it is a stretch (Hurka, 2014a: 145–6). Sidgwick mentions the phrase "from the point of view of the universe" only three times in the *Methods* (ME xx, 382, 420) and in only one of the philosophical intuitions (P). In the places Sidgwick mentions RB he does not suggest it should be read as stating what is true only from the point of view of the universe. He presents it as telling us what we ought, as a rational being, to do (SE 411; FC 483; GSM 124, 128; ME 404, 418).

Second, Sidgwick seems to reject a similar interpretation of the maxim of prudence. When discussing O, he focuses on one's good on the whole, or what is good from the point of view of one's life as a whole. From this point of view, he says, no one moment in one's life is more intrinsically important than any other unless there are grounds for thinking that more good is likely to be realized in one moment than in another (ME 381). He does not seem to think an opponent of O could agree to O because it states only what is true from the point of one's life as a whole, and then decline to take up this point of view. Sidgwick seems to think it is rationally required to take up this point of view.

---

[28] For a defence of Sidgwick's hedonism, see de Lazari-Radek and Singer, 2014: chs. 8–9; for a reply to Ross in specific, see de Lazari-Radek and Singer, 2014: 283–4.

Sidgwick likely accorded RB the same or similar status.

Sidgwick cannot, we have seen, clearly establish the superiority of his philosophical intuitions over the apparent intuitions in common sense that he takes great strides to attack. His case for utilitarianism might therefore be doomed.

He could reply to concerns targeting his intuitions by relying more heavily on the proof of utilitarianism he offers to the proponent of common-sense morality. According to this proof, utilitarianism's capacity to support, clarify, and systematize the main rules of common sense in a manner generally agreeable to the proponent of common sense offers the proponent rational considerations to accept utilitarianism (ME 421–2). Proving utilitarianism involves demonstrating how it

> not only supports broadly the current moral rules, but also sustains their generally received limitations and qualifications: that, again, it explains anomalies in the Morality of Common Sense, which from any other point of view must seem unsatisfactory to the reflective intellect; and moreover, where the current formula is not sufficiently precise for the guidance of conduct, while at the same time difficulties and perplexities arise in the attempt to give it additional precision, the Utilitarian method solves these difficulties and perplexities in general accordance with the vague instincts of Common Sense, and is naturally appealed to for such solution in ordinary moral discussions. (ME 425)

It is possible to grasp utilitarianism's relationship to common-sense morality by examining utilitarianism's capacity to support the importance of veracity and to solve its infelicities in ways common sense vaguely accepts:

> the general utility of truth-speaking [is] so manifest as to need no proof, but wherever this utility seems to be absent, or outweighed by particular bad consequences, we find that Common Sense at least hesitates to enforce the rule. For example, if a man be pursuing criminal ends, it is *prima facie* injurious to the community that he should be aided in his pursuit by being able to rely on the assertions of others. Here, then, deception is *prima facie* legitimate as a protection against crime: though when we consider the bad effects on habit, and through example, of even a single act of unveracity, the case is seen to be, on Utilitarian principles, doubtful: and this is just the view of Common Sense. Again, though it is generally a man's interest to know the truth, there are exceptional cases in which it is injurious to him – as when an invalid hears bad news – and here, too, Common Sense is disposed to suspend the rule. Again, we found it difficult to define exactly wherein Veracity consists; for we may either require truth in the spoken words, or in the inferences which the speaker foresees will be drawn from them, or in both. Perfect Candour, no doubt, would require it in both: but in the various circumstances where this seems inexpedient, we often find Common Sense at least half-willing to dispense with one or other part of the double obligation. Thus we found ... the unsuitability of perfect frankness to our existing social relations is recognised in the common rules of politeness, which impose on us not unfrequently the necessity of suppressing truths and suggesting

> falsehoods. I would not say that in any of these cases Common Sense pronounces
> quite decidedly in favour of unveracity: but then neither is Utilitarianism decided,
> as the utility of maintaining a general habit of truth-speaking is so great, that it is
> not easy to prove it to be clearly outweighed by even strong special reasons for
> violating the rule. (ME 448–9)

Sidgwick is careful to disclaim complete coincidence between common-sense morality and utilitarianism (ME 455–6, 463–7, 497; IE 34–5). Utilitarianism and common-sense morality will conflict in some cases; in such cases

> there will remain some discrepancy in details between our particular moral
> sentiments and unreasoned judgments on the one hand, and the apparent results
> of special utilitarian calculations on the other; and we may often have some
> practical difficulty in balancing the latter against the more general utilitarian
> reasons for obeying the former: but there seems to be no longer any theoretical
> perplexity as to the principles for determining social duty. (ME 497)

Sidgwick's proof is, of course, open to doubt in some cases. Common sense thinks it morally permissible (and in some cases obligatory) to prioritize the happiness of those near and dear (partners, children, friends, and so on) relative to strangers. Common sense

> seems rather to regard it as immediately certain without any such deduction
> [from utilitarianism] that we owe special dues of kindness to those who stand
> in special relations to us. (ME 242)

Utilitarianism may capture aspects of this common-sense view. Sidgwick is an indirect utilitarian: the best way to promote general happiness is to pursue it indirectly rather than directly (ME 85–6, 413, 490). General happiness is promoted most effectively if we aim at something other than general happiness. His case is helped if common-sense morality is, as he maintains, inchoately and unconsciously utilitarian and if there is a "general presumption which evolution afforded that moral sentiments and opinions would point to conduct conducive to general happiness" (ME xxiii). He says in practice the promotion of general happiness is achieved best when

> each man, even with a view to universal Good … chiefly … [concerns]
> himself with promoting the good of a limited number of human beings, and
> that generally in proportion to the closeness of their connection with him.
> (ME 382; also ME 241–2)

and when

> each individual … [distributes] his beneficence in the channels marked out by
> commonly recognised ties and claims … the domestic, and those constituted
> by consanguinity, friendship, previous kindness, and special needs. (ME 433)

Utilitarianism may in this way capture the partiality important to common-sense morality, though Sidgwick's confidence is not entirely warranted in view of the problems plaguing utilitarian calculations that he foregrounds (ME 414; FC 485–6). He does not show conclusively how partiality in practice will *maximize* general happiness. In any case, he is certainly not warranted in asserting

> that a 'plain man,' in a modern civilised society, if his conscience were fairly brought to consider the hypothetical question, whether it would be morally right for him to seek his own happiness on any occasion if it involved a certain sacrifice of the greater happiness of some other human being, – without any counterbalancing gain to any one else, – would answer unhesitatingly in the negative. (ME 382)

Even his fans express skepticism. Parfit calls this claim "simply false" (Parfit, 2011: 453). Sidgwick does explain that

> we conceive it as the aim of a philosopher, as such, to do somewhat more than define and formulate the common moral opinions of mankind. His function is to tell men what they ought to think, rather than what they do think: he is expected to transcend Common Sense in his premises, and is allowed a certain divergence from Common Sense in his conclusions. (ME 373; IE 34–5)

Divergence has limits, but whether and how he falls within them is left unclear. The conclusions Sidgwick draws from his utilitarianism are a mixed bag. In politics, for example, he endorses socialistic policies and egalitarian forms of redistribution (EP 143–78; ES) but also British imperialism and colonization more generally (EP 298–328; PE 102–3).[29] He leaves us skeptical about what actually follows from utilitarianism. This is perhaps unsurprising given that the results of utilitarian calculations are "doubtful and difficult" (ME 87).

In this section, we explored Sidgwick's case for utilitarianism. The *Methods* concludes claiming that rational egoism and utilitarianism represent coordinate but conflicting requirements of rationality. Utilitarianism is only half of this so-called "dualism of practical reason." We have yet to see Sidgwick's argument for egoism. This is the topic of the next section.

5 The Case for Rational Egoism and the Dualism of Practical Reason

This section grapples with Sidgwick's case for thinking egoism is as compelling as utilitarianism and therefore there is a dualism of practical reason.

---

[29] For discussion of Sidgwick's socialism and imperialism, see Schultz, 2004, 2005; for the criticism that Sidgwick's politics is in general conservative, see Miller, 2020.

Sidgwick did not end the *Methods* concerned about the relationship between common-sense morality and utilitarianism. Instead, in the book's Concluding Chapter he regrets being unable to rationally reconcile utilitarianism and rational egoism. The latter view, recall, is that

> the rational agent regards quantity of consequent pleasure and pain to himself as alone important in choosing between alternatives of action; and seeks always the greatest attainable surplus of pleasure over pain – which ... we may designate as his 'greatest happiness.' (ME 95; also 121)

The problem confronting Sidgwick at the conclusion of the *Methods* is the lack of practical coincidence between rational egoism and utilitarianism. The difficulty is that in some cases what maximizes general happiness is not what maximizes the individual's happiness. Suppose Bloggs has some medicine. Bloggs comes down with an illness which will cause him mild pain for a few months, after which time he will recover fully. If he takes the medicine, he can prevent the pain. Jones has a more severe form of the same illness. His pain over the next few months will be much worse. Before Bloggs became ill he promised the medicine to Jones (who has no power to harm Bloggs if Bloggs fails to fulfill his promise). Utilitarianism says Bloggs ought to give the medicine to Jones, for the benefit to Jones is greater, and Bloggs promised. Egoism says he ought to keep it for himself. Egoism forbids what utilitarianism demands.

Sidgwick considers two strategies for reconciling egoism and utilitarianism. First, imagine Bloggs is a very sympathetic character and so his happiness depends on Jones' (ME 500). This might, Sidgwick says, close the gap between egoism and utilitarian in the above case. Unfortunately, Sidgwick reports, cases exist in which even the most sympathetic egoist will recoil from the utilitarian option:

> Suppose a man finds that a regard for the general good – Utilitarian Duty – demands from him a sacrifice, or extreme risk, of life. There are perhaps one or two human beings so dear to him that the remainder of a life saved by sacrificing their happiness to his own would be worthless to him from an egoistic point of view. But it is doubtful whether many men, "sitting down in a cool hour" to make the estimate, would affirm even this: and of course that particular portion of the general happiness, for which one is called upon to sacrifice one's own, may easily be the happiness of person's not especially dear to one. (ME 502)

Second, Sidgwick suggests that God might, if he is assumed to exist, produce (practical) coincidence between egoism and utilitarianism. God could reward the egoist for obeying utilitarian edicts and punish her for failing to do so (at least in the afterlife). He does not deny God's existence (M 228). He is tempted in places to embrace theism because it introduces greater system into practical reason (M 605). Nevertheless, he declares himself unable to find an intuition that God will reward compliance and punish non-compliance with utilitarianism and so he rejects this reconciliation strategy (ME 507).

It might be possible to overcome this conflict by referring to a more basic rational perspective from which to adjudicate it. But, for Sidgwick, there is no such perspective.[30] At most, we can appeal to a non-rational preference for one view over the other (ME 508; FC 485). Reason is, then, unable to tell us what we ought, all things considered, to do in these cases. In the absence of any rational way to decide the conflict, we are forced, Sidgwick says,

> to admit an ultimate and fundamental contradiction in our apparent intuitions of what is Reasonable in conduct; and from this admission it would seem to follow that the apparently intuitive operation of the Practical Reason, manifested in these contradictory judgements, is after all illusory. (ME 508)

The attempt to find a unique method of ethics for rationally determining what we ought to do therefore ends in failure (ME1 473). Sidgwick is unable to improve the plight of the plain person who asks: why should I do what I see to be right? He leaves us with a plurality of methods and no rational way for deciding between them. If we are unable to demonstrate a "harmony" between rational egoism and utilitarianism, he says, morality cannot be made "completely rational" (ME 498; also 508). Hence, we are left with a dualism of practical reason, the "profoundest problem of Ethics" (ME 386n4).

In order to see how Sidgwick arrives at the dualism, we must now examine his argument for egoism.

Sidgwick suggests that the conflict between egoism and utilitarianism reveals a contradiction in our philosophical intuitions. From what has been argued above, it may be obvious that the conflict, for Sidgwick, is between the philosophical intuitions O and RB. However, Sidgwick is not always clear on this.

In a passage referenced previously, he claims

> It would be contrary to Common Sense to deny that the distinction between any one individual and any other is real and fundamental, and that consequently "I" am concerned with the quality of my existence as an individual in a sense, fundamentally important, in which I am not concerned with the quality of the existence of other individuals: and this being so, I do not see how it can be proved that this distinction is not to be taken as fundamental in determining the ultimate end of rational action for an individual. (ME 498; also FC 484)

---

[30] For criticism of this, see Parfit, 2011: 134–6.

It is certainly true that Sidgwick's case for egoism relies in part on appeal to the distinction between individuals.[31] After all, without such a distinction the view cannot get off the ground. We can draw a clear line, he thinks, between self and others (e.g., my point of view and others' point of view). The distinction seems, for Sidgwick's egoist, of utmost practical significance. It plays a pivotal role in their view about the proper distribution of rational concern. As noted previously, Sidgwick admits to failing to provide in the first few editions of the *Methods* "sufficient rational justification, so far as Egoism is concerned" (FC 484). Some support is provided, he seems to suggest, by appeal to the distinction between individuals (FC 484). Sidgwick says it is self-evident that the "distinction is to be taken as fundamental in determining the ultimate end of rational action for an individual" (FC 484), though it "contradicts the equally self-evident proposition that my own good is no more to be regarded than the good of another" (FC 484).[32]

This provides a view of the conflict and a possible argument for egoism. The conflict is between the intuition regarding the reality and fundamentality of the distinction and the practical importance of it to establishing rational aims (which, for Sidgwick's egoist, involves affirming exclusive concern for one's own happiness) and rational benevolence (the presupposition of which is presumably that the distinction between individuals is, though real and fundamental, not practically important to determining rational aims for an individual). The dispute is not over the metaphysical fact of the distinction between individuals; it is over its normative import (FC 485). An argument for egoism based on the distinction may take the following form (Phillips, 2011: 127–8):

1. The distinction between any one individual and any other is real and fundamental.
2. If the distinction between any one individual and any other is real and fundamental, then I ought to be concerned with the quality of my existence as an individual in a sense, fundamentally important, in which I ought not to be concerned with the quality of the existence of other individuals.
3. Therefore, I ought to be concerned with the quality of my existence as an individual in a sense, fundamentally important, in which I ought not to be concerned with the quality of the existence of other individuals.

An argument of this sort will not support egoism. First, P2 is problematic. To arrive at a normative conclusion P2 is interpreted to include a claim about what ought to

---

[31] Sidgwick first introduced the claim about the distinction between individuals in FC in 1889 in reply to the criticism that he had not previously provided egoism with sufficient justification. The distinction claim was later incorporated into ME4 in 1890 and then appeared in all subsequent editions of the *Methods*.

[32] He does not say this in the *Methods* when he discusses the distinction passage (ME 498).

concern one rather than about what will concern one. It says given the fact of metaphysical distinctness and one's relationship to certain goods (bads) (e.g., pains and pleasures one directly experiences), one ought to be concerned with the quality of one's own existence more than with the quality of others' existence. This suggests the possibility of (rationally) transitioning from is (the distinction between individuals and one's connection to certain goods and bads) to ought (normatively greater concern for one's self). However, as noted above, Sidgwick denies the legitimacy of reasoning from is to ought (SE 412; FP 107; ME 98, 388; PE 68; PSR 237).

Second, the argument does not secure *exclusive* concern for one's own good (which Phillips, 2011: 128–9 allows). It will not suffice to support the strong claim that concern with one's own good ought to be exclusive and so will not justify completely the irrationality of uncompensated sacrifice (FC 484). Phillips rightly points out that at best all the argument gets Sidgwick is the existence of "genuine agent-relative reasons" (Phillips, 2011: 129). But the argument does not really secure even these such reasons; instead, it seems in P2 to involve asserting that such reasons exist given separateness. The argument seems even on Phillips's rendering to involve little more than assertion. As he puts it, "How could the fact that something has a special effect on *me* not affect *my* reasons?" (Phillips, 2011: 129; italics in original).

Third, thinking that this is *the* argument for egoism ignores that the distinction between individuals is not all Sidgwick relies on to support egoism. He uses it mainly to deflect the worry he supplied insufficient rational justification of egoism and its assumptions.[33] Appeal to the distinction between individuals is more plausibly thought of as supplementing the case for egoism rather than operating as the major premise in the argument for it.

It is possible that Sidgwick means to suggest that the distinction between individuals implies commitment to the irrationality of sacrificing one's own good for the greater benefit of others without compensation. David Brink says

> Sidgwick supposes that because we are separate persons, with different lives to lead, it is unreasonable to demand *uncompensated sacrifices* of agents. Because we are separate persons, I am not compensated when I undergo a sacrifice for a greater benefit to you; your gains cannot make up to me for my losses. Sidgwick's appeal to the separateness of persons implicitly invokes this principle that the *rationality* of sacrifice requires compensation. (Brink, 1992: 209; italics in original)

---

[33] In ME, Sidgwick suggests that the distinction is important to avoiding the proof (discussed below) that he tries to deploy to move the rational egoist to utilitarianism (ME 497–8).

This interpretation of Sidgwick has some plausibility. Sidgwick says, for example, before introducing the distinction between individuals, that the conflict or dualism results because

> Along with (a) a fundamental moral conviction that I ought to sacrifice my own happiness, if by so doing I can increase the happiness of others to a greater extent than I diminish my own, I find also (b) a conviction ... that it would be irrational to sacrifice any portion of my own happiness unless the sacrifice is to be somehow at some time compensated by an equivalent addition to my own happiness. I find both these fundamental convictions in my own thought with as much clearness and certainty as the process of introspective reflection can give. (FC 483)

But this interpretation of Sidgwick has two flaws. First, like Phillips, Brink interprets Sidgwick as moving from is to ought (or from is to what is unreasonable).[34] Second, Sidgwick's mention of the distinction between individuals might well invoke the claim respecting sacrifice requiring compensation. But this does not explain how the distinction passage buttresses the irrationality of uncompensated sacrifice. The claim about the illegitimacy of uncompensated sacrifice is more plausibly thought of as implying or invoking separateness rather than being implied by it, in which case we need an argument for the illegitimacy of uncompensated sacrifice.

Appeal to the distinction between individuals will not alone support egoism.[35] We need more than it to secure the irrationality of uncompensated sacrifice. It is more fruitful to seek an argument for egoism in which the distinction between individuals plays only (and at best) a supporting or supplemental role. As noted, Sidgwick repeatedly says the dualism of practical reason involves a contradiction in our intuitions (ME 418, 508; FC 483–4). He says at one point that:

> even if a man admits the self-evidence of the principle of Rational Benevolence, he may still hold that his own happiness is an end which it is irrational for him to sacrifice to any other; and that therefore a harmony between the maxim of Prudence and the maxim of Rational Benevolence must be somehow demonstrated, if morality is to be made completely rational. (ME 498)

It is plausible, then, that at the core of the dualism and what gives rise to it is a tension between the Maxim of Prudence or O and the Maxim of Rational Benevolence or RB. The two methods based on them – rational egoism and utilitarianism – in some cases deliver conflicting practical directives, leaving us with no rational determination of what to do.

Sidgwick's discussion of egoism takes place in Book II of the *Methods*. He offers some considerations in favour of the view, to which we will turn shortly. However, his main preoccupation is the potential intrinsic "impracticability of

---

[34] Parfit, 2011: 133 does the same.

[35] For the same conclusion, see Schultz, 2004: 216; Shaver, 2020.

Hedonism" as a rational method that involves comparing and aggregating pleasures (and pains) (ME 132). In this context, he discusses impediments to precision in judgements about the quantitative relations between pleasures and pains (required for determining which of one's options conduces to the greatest possible surplus of pleasure over pain for one) and the viability of methods other than the empirical method for use in figuring out one's own good on the whole.

To construct an argument for egoism we must look elsewhere.[36] In light of what I have said above, the best place to begin is with O or the axiom (maxim) of prudence that Sidgwick offers in Book III, ch. xiii:

> One ought to aim at one's own good on the whole, not merely at a particular
> part of it, giving equal weight to equal quantities of good (ME 381).

It might be possible to get from O to rational egoism through a route similar to the one Sidgwick takes to get from RB to utilitarianism. The argument of Book III, ch. xiii establishes RB as only one moral axiom or principle, not the sole axiom. This leaves room for other axioms, including O. Sidgwick thinks, as we noted, hedonism is established in Book III, ch. xiv:

> Happiness is the sole ultimate good (ME 406).

From O and H, we get

> One ought to aim at one's own happiness on the whole, not merely at
> a particular part of it, giving equal weight to equal quantities of happiness.

Let us call this E. E is the first principle of egoism. When Sidgwick argues from HRB to utilitarianism proper he relies in part on the argument that an investigation of common-sense morality furnishes no (apparent) intuitive truths; its main principles are subordinate and derivative. Sidgwick might make a similar move when arguing from E to rational egoism. He says at one point that his argument that the rules of common-sense morality fail to satisfy the conditions for highest certainty "leads us to regard other moral rules as subordinate to the principles of Prudence and Benevolence" (ME 384). He might maintain, putting aside HRB, that since there are no other principles in common-sense morality competing with E, we may move to

> One ought to aim only at one's own happiness on the whole, not merely at
> a particular part of it, giving equal weight to equal quantities of happiness.

---

[36] For a different argument than the one given here, see Schneewind, 1977: 361–66; this argument involves construing B in a way that supports egoism.

There are, then, parallel arguments for egoism and utilitarianism, each involving appeal to a philosophical intuition, O and RB, respectively, and proceeding to each method through a defence of hedonism and a rejection of competing normative principles (other than each other). Like the utilitarian, the egoist will have to provide arguments for some of its unique features, including maximization. Egoism and utilitarianism conflict in practice in part because the philosophical intuitions on which they rest are in tension with each other.

As in the case of utilitarianism, the case for egoism is further developed by showcasing its power to systematize some of our common-sense prudential and moral attitudes (Schneewind, 1977: 358–61; Shaver, 1999: 99ff.). Common sense has developed, Sidgwick thinks, an inventory of sources of individual happiness, including

> health, wealth, friendship and family affections, fame and social position, power, interesting and congenial occupation and amusement, – including the gratification, in some form, of the love of knowledge, and of those refined, partly sensual, partly emotional, susceptibilities which we call aesthetic. (ME 153)

Sidgwick admits that common sense might provide something "tolerably coherent" for the purpose of figuring out what will make one happy (ME 158). But to clarify and adjudicate conflicts between the items in its inventory common sense requires some other method which, Sidgwick suggests, rational egoism might supply (ME 157). In addition, egoism might serve to capture and explain some aspects of common-sense morality. He seems to admit that in general acting on the norms of common-sense morality conduces to one's own happiness (FC 485; ME 175), though, unsurprisingly, he agrees, as with utilitarianism, that egoism will conflict with common-sense morality in various cases (ME 175, 498–9). (We will return to this below.)

Sidgwick attempts to buttress the case for egoism in three further ways. First, he argues the rational egoist can resist the proof of utilitarianism Sidgwick offers. As noted, he attempts to prove utilitarianism to common-sense morality. He thinks his proof succeeds. It involves (recall)

> a line of argument which on the one hand allows the validity, to a certain extent, of the maxims already accepted, and on the other hand shows them to be not absolutely valid, but needing to be controlled and completed by some more comprehensive principle. (ME 420)

Sidgwick thinks this line succeeds only with the less-than-savvy egoist who believes that happiness is good not only from her point of view, but from the point of view of the universe. It is possible to lead the less-than-savvy egoist from this belief to utilitarianism by clarifying that her happiness cannot be a more important part of the general good than any other part (FP 107). If one takes it as rational to pursue one's happiness because it is good from the point of view of the universe, one has reason to pursue others' happiness since others' happiness is no less good than one's own from this point of view (ME 421, 497).

Utilitarianism cannot, however, be proven to the savvy egoist who may avoid the proof by asserting only that her happiness is good for her from her point of view. Since "it cannot be proved that the difference between . . . [the egoist's] own happiness and another's happiness is not *for* . . . *[her]* all-important," utilitarianism cannot be proved to the savvy egoist (ME 420; italics in original; also 497).

Second, he argues that the egoist can fend off an attack on an assumption of her view, that "the distinction between any one individual and any other is real and fundamental" (FC 484; ME 498). Sidgwick considers a critic who denies the reality and therefore the importance of the distinction between individuals. It has been suggested that Sidgwick has Schopenhauer in mind as the critic (Shaver, 2020: 445–6).[37] Sidgwick describes his view as follows:

> it is One Will that is the innermost essence of every thing and of the totality of things. This Will, by its very nature, strives blindly to manifest and objectify itself . . . But as this striving necessarily implies defect and discontent with the present condition, the life which it constitutes and maintains is essentially a suffering life . . . In this unhappy state of things the duty that philosophy points out to man is plainly the negation or denial of will; in this all true morality is summed up . . . [obtaining virtue involves] a recognition of the real identity of any one ego with all others; the virtuous man represses and denies the egoism from which all injustice springs. (OHE 280–1)

Rational egoism assumes that there must be an individual – me – distinct from other individuals whose happiness may be sacrificed for my benefit. Sidgwick's assertion that the distinction between individuals is the "assumption" on which egoism is based seems positioned to block this objection (FC 484). If this assumption is accepted, it is possible to embrace O and for the egoist to claim her happiness is for her all-important and that it remains rational, then, for her to pursue her happiness (potentially) at a cost to others' happiness. Sidgwick is confident in this assumption perhaps because common-sense morality (not to mention some philosophers (FC 483–4)) commit to something like it in embracing E (ME 7, 119–20, 199, 419).

As we noted, Sidgwick seems at points to draw normative conclusions from the distinction between individuals. He appears to tie the reality and fundamentality of the distinction between individuals to the irrationality of uncompensated sacrifice (FC 484–5). Inferring the latter from the former involves a very strong claim about the practical significance of the distinction between individuals. Sidgwick admits he cannot prove the practical significance of the

---

[37] For the claim that Hume is the objector, see Brink, 1992: 208; Shaver, 1999: 84–5.

distinction between individuals to those who refuse to admit it, though he, himself, finds such a refusal "impossible" (FC 485). Drawing normative conclusions from the distinction between persons is not plausible. However, it is plausible to rely on the distinction between individuals to deflect a possible objection to rational egoism.

Third, Sidgwick argues that his rational egoism might be able to fend off challenges from rival forms of egoism. Rational egoism is open to objection not only from those denying the distinction between individuals, but from a different breed of egoist. Rational egoism says one ought to aim only at one's own good on the whole. To whom a benefit or burden falls is all-important to the rational egoist, but the time at which it falls in one's life is not directly relevant. Rational egoism is person relative, but time neutral (Parfit, 1984: 140–1; Brink, 1992: 200). A rival to egoism might embrace its commitment to person relativity but reject its commitment to time neutrality. This brand of egoism would be person *and* time relative. Parfit calls this the present-aim view, which

> tells each to do what will best achieve his *present* aims (Parfit, 1984: 92; italics added).

Sidgwick confronts this form of egoism. He expresses the challenge it poses to rational egoism as follows:

> I do not see why the axiom of Prudence should not be questioned, when it conflicts with present inclination, on a ground similar to that on which Egoists refuse to admit the axiom of Rational Benevolence. If the Utilitarian has to answer the question, 'Why should I sacrifice my own happiness for the greater happiness of another?' it must surely be admissible to ask the Egoist, 'Why should I sacrifice a present pleasure for a greater one in the future? Why should I concern myself about my own future feelings any more than about the feelings of other persons?' (ME 418)

Rational egoism says if forgoing a present (surplus) good for me now produces a greater (surplus) good for me in the future, the sacrifice is rationally required. This maximizes my good considering my life as a whole. My present self might, however, balk and demand justification for the sacrifice. A demand of this sort might seem absurd. After all, the one making the sacrifice and the one benefitting appear one and the same. There is, then, no uncompensated sacrifice. Sidgwick explains how the demand for such justification cannot be "repudiated as absurd" (ME 418) by the followers of Hume who "[g]rant that the Ego is merely a system of coherent phenomena, that the permanent identical 'I' is not a fact but a fiction" (ME 419). If Hume and his followers are right, Sidgwick says, and the ego is "resolved" into a series of feelings, we might ask why the series of feelings comprising my present self should sacrifice for the series of feelings comprising my future self.

Sidgwick declines to "press" the objection against rational egoism, because "[c]ommon [s]ense does not think it worth while to supply the individual with reasons for seeking his own interest" (ME 419). He is presumably assuming the common-sense normative view includes commitment to the distinction between individuals and to the "I" being permanent, a fact not a fiction.[38] Common sense does not think it worth whole to supply individuals with reasons to seek their own good *on the whole.*

Sidgwick might have done a bit more here. On Sidgwick's reading, Humeans deny the existence of something in consciousness that stays the same over time (e.g., a soul). For them, an individual is "merely" a system of coherent phenomena, or a series of feelings.[39] But it is not clear what follows from this respecting reasons for action. It is not clear why one part of an individual would not sacrifice for another part even given Hume's view (as Sidgwick sees it). Sidgwick might be thinking that Humeans hold that the relations between the series of feelings or mental states making up an individual now and at a later time may not be strongly connected enough to warrant sacrifice of the present good of an individual for the greater good of its future self. Humeans might seem, then, to claim that there is just a series of feelings existing at any one time and when psychological connections (desires, beliefs, memories) between them and future such series are weak, the sacrifice of an individual's present good for future benefit looks suspect (Parfit, 1984: 313). It might be difficult to meet this claim with mere assertion about what common sense thinks.

Sidgwick has two options here. First, he may be able to shop around for a well-defended view of personal identity fitting with egoism and rely on it.[40] Second, he might argue that *because* we have an unshakable confidence in the claim that we have reason to seek our own good on the whole, we have good reason therefore to *assume* a theory of personal identity undergirding it. The egoist might rely on an idea expressed by Rawls, on which "the conclusions of the philosophy of mind regarding the question of personal identity do not provide grounds for accepting one of the leading moral conceptions rather than another. Whatever these conclusions are, intuitionism and utilitarianism,

---

[38] For discussion of the potential impact of Sidgwick's psychical or paranormal research on this aspect of his view, see Schultz, 2017: 276–301. Schultz argues that Sidgwick's research in this domain revealed the self to be less unified than we might otherwise have thought, since the research revealed that there were conscious and subliminal elements within the human personality, making reductionist or Humean views more compelling. Schultz thinks Sidgwick may have made little use of psychical research in his philosophical works because "he may well have worried, in his usual way, that more selves might also mean more conflicts and divisions within reason, with the dualism becoming a multiplex of practical reason that would be even more intractable" (Schultz, 2017: 294). But it is equally likely that he worried that any conclusion he might draw based on his research would be premature.

[39] In places, Sidgwick interprets Hume as committed to "the impossibility of finding a self in the stream of psychical experience" (LK 453; also 454).

[40] One might be found in Sullivan, 2018: 68.

perfectionist and Kantian views, can each use a criterion of identity that accords with them" (Rawls, 1974: 15).

But it is open to the person- and time-relative egoist to admit the distinction between persons and that the permanent "I" is a fact not a fiction and still reject rational egoism. Such an egoist could deny the practical significance of permanence. In this case, the egoist might, if it is the present-aim normative view they are following, argue we ought to maximize what we at present most want or value.

Sidgwick is not well placed to rebut this view. He might try to argue that desires are not the kind of thing that one ought to promote. He notes in various places that desires frequently lead us astray (ME 7, 41–2, 58, 153, 241). This will not suffice, however. The present-aim theory may take the form of what Parfit calls the critical present-aim view, on which one ought to do "whatever will best achieve those of . . . [one's] present aims that are not irrational" or that survive a process of deliberation (Parfit, 1984: 94; also 119). The best Sidgwick can do in reply is insist that the arguments for this version of the present-aim view are no more plausible than his arguments for rational egoism.

Let us turn now to criticisms. The argument for egoism is susceptible to some of the criticisms made of the argument for utilitarianism, including the criticisms that the intuitions on which it relies do not qualify as higher certainties because they are not clear and precise in practice and that it cannot establish common-sense morality as derivative and dependent. The argument is also open to distinct objections, three of which will be raised here.

First, Sidgwick permits the egoist to confine direct concern to only her own happiness (ME 420). One might wonder whether it is arbitrary to confine one's attention in this way (Shaver, 1999: 86, 90–3). Sidgwick dismisses various views because they are arbitrary.[41] Let's focus on some notable examples.

Sidgwick grants non-human animals moral standing (ME 241, 414, 431). He insists that failure to take into account the happiness of non-human animals "seems arbitrary and unreasonable" (ME 414; also FP 107). He does not regard differences in rationality or (presumably) species membership as grounds for differences in ethical treatment (FP 107).[42]

Sidgwick thinks it is impermissible in theory to confine one's attention to the well-being of one's family or one's nation alone (ME 10; PE 68; EP 299). We remarked on this in the first section. Sidgwick says it might be

---

[41] For Sidgwick a distinction is arbitrary when "no sufficient reason can be given" for it (ME 267–8).

[42] Sidgwick drew less than radical practical conclusions from his extension of moral standing to non-human animals (see EP 141–2). Here as elsewhere he seemingly fails to grasp the true implications of his utilitarianism. For more radical conclusions respecting our obligations to non-human animals based on Sidgwickian principles, see Singer, 2011, chs. 3–5. For criticism of Sidgwick on non-human animals, see Irwin, 2009: 395, 485, 513.

> possible to adopt an end intermediate between the two [individual and general happiness], and to aim at the happiness of some limited portion of mankind, such as one's family or nation or race[43]: but any such limitation seems arbitrary, and probably few would maintain it to be reasonable *per se*, except as the most practicable way of aiming at the general happiness, or of indirectly securing one's own. (ME 10)

Sidgwick has a particular distaste for what he calls "national egoism" (PE 65). In his *Elements* he says

> It is sometimes frankly affirmed, and more often implied, in discussions on the principles of foreign policy, that a State is not properly subject – as an individual is commonly held to be – to any restraint of duty limiting the pursuit of its own interest: that its own interest is, necessarily and properly, its paramount end; and that when we affirm that it is bound to conform to any rules of international duty we can only mean, or ought only to mean, that such conformity will – on the whole and in the long run if not immediately – be conducive to its national interests. In my view all such statements are essentially immoral. (EP 298–9; also PE 67–8)

He does not exactly say why national egoism is immoral. He gives an argument elsewhere suggesting his concern is tied in part to arbitrariness.

> I have never seen, nor can I conceive, any ethical reasoning that will provide even a plausible basis for the compound proposition that a man is bound to sacrifice his private interest to that of the group of human beings constituting his state, but that neither he nor they are under any similar obligation to the rest of mankind. (PE 68)

Sidgwick is convinced that it would be arbitrary to deny non-instrumental value to the happiness of non-human animals, non-family members, and non-co-nationals, if you take the happiness of humans, family members, and co-nationals to be non-instrumentally good. What makes happiness an object of concern is its being happiness, not being the happiness of my species, my family members, or my co-nationals.

He is, however, unconvinced that egoism is arbitrary. He raises the following challenge to egoism:

> I may start with the egoistic maxim that "it is reasonable for me to take my own greatest happiness as the ultimate end of my conduct"; and then may yield to the argument that the happiness of any other individual, equally capable and deserving of happiness, must be no less worth aiming at than my own; and thus may come to accept the utilitarian maxim that "happiness generally is to be sought" as the real first principle; considering the egoistic maxim to be only true in so far as it is a partial and subordinate expression of this latter. (FP 107)

---

[43] For Sidgwick's troubling views on race and compelling evidence of racism, see Schultz 2005.

He does not yield to this challenge, even though he suggests egoism might be "arbitrary and without foundation in reason" (FP 107). Why is it arbitrary to confine my attention to the happiness of my fellow species members, my co-nationals or my family alone, but not arbitrary to confine attention to my own happiness alone? What is the difference between my happiness and the happiness of my nation or of my family? Sidgwick does not seem to have a good answer. Indeed, his application of the charge of arbitrariness threatens to be arbitrary itself. If he can be accused of unfairness in his argument for utilitarianism, he can most certainly be accused of unfairness in his argument for egoism. He treats some views limiting impartial concern more harshly than others.

Sidgwick's arbitrariness charge appears persuasive in the cases he considers in part because he construes the positions he attacks in very implausible ways. When criticizing national egoism, he points out how odd it would be to argue that one should sacrifice (without compensation) to promote one's nation's happiness but not to promote the happiness of any other members of humankind. Sidgwick might use the same argument against the views confining one's attention to the happiness of one's family or one's species.

But, as suggested previously, we need not follow Sidgwick in how we construe the positions. An exponent of partiality to one's family or one's nation might argue that we are permitted to give some extra weight to the happiness of our co-nationals or family members, though not exclusive concern. These views do not seem obviously arbitrary. Sidgwick may not bother with views of this variety because they appear unsystematic. He rather flippantly declares, without clear proof, that partial views may be absorbed by egoism or utilitarianism.

When compared with the more plausible versions of the views Sidgwick rejects as arbitrary, egoism looks implausibly strong. At the very least, it requires more defence than Sidgwick allows. It is arbitrary to confine all your attention to the happiness of your family or your nation because the happiness of others seems like it provides reasons in the same way your family's or nation's happiness provides reasons. That one is a member of your family or your nation is not robust enough to support exclusive concern for your family or nation. One might argue that the fact that your happiness is yours is not robust enough to support exclusive concern for yourself.

Let's turn now to a second criticism of egoism. The criticism we have just considered may not impugn egoism completely. It might be true that we ought to promote our own happiness even if it is false we ought to promote *only* our own happiness. Rational egoism might be challenged, but E might stand. E seems a very plausible claim. But many disagree with E. It may therefore fail test 4 of Sidgwick's epistemic conditions discussed in Section 2. It is important to note that, for Sidgwick, E is a requirement distinct from utilitarianism and beneficence. In commenting on Kant's account of the duty of beneficence, Sidgwick says for Kant one has a duty to seek one's own happiness only when one considers it "as a part of the happiness of mankind in general" (ME 386; for Kant's claim, see 1997b: 5:34). He disagrees with Kant, he says, thinking (with Butler) that seeking one's own happiness is an obligation "independently of one's relation to other men" (ME 386). In this case, I might be permitted to favour myself when all other considerations are tied.[44]

One of Sidgwick's "masters" is Kant (ME xx). He was more than aware that Kant offered a number of ways of dealing with the conflict between duty and self-interest. In the first edition of the *Methods* Sidgwick rejects Kant's practical postulation of a God to reconcile duty with individual happiness (Kant, 1997b: 5:124ff) as no more than a "momentary half-wilful irrationality, committed in a violent access of philosophic despair" (ME1 471; also ME 507n3; M 615; cf. GSM 188; M 467). The appeal to a postulate is, however, not the only tool one might borrow from Kant for overcoming a dualism of practical reason.

Sidgwick concedes Kant is not using the practical postulate to solve the dualism, since the latter "does not mean to recognise the principle of Egoism as rational" (ME1 471 n; also ME 36, 327n1, 366, 386; Kant, 2002: 5:386; Kant, 1997b: 5:93). Kant could avoid a dualism of practical reason in part by denying categorical requirements of prudence. Kant *apparently* denies E. In defending RB Sidgwick appeals to Kant for support, though he attacks Kant's manner of grounding something like RB (ME 389-9n). Sidgwick does not contend with Kant's arguments against E despite thinking of Kant as an expert in connection with epistemic condition 4 described in Section 2.

Kant provides numerous arguments against an obligation to promote one's own happiness. One says we cannot have a direct duty to promote our own happiness because everyone as a matter of fact wills their own happiness, and "[w]hat everyone already wants unavoidably, of his own accord, does not come under the concept of *duty*, which is *constraint* to an end adopted reluctantly" (Kant, 1996: 6:386; also 1996: 6:451).

This is not a very persuasive argument. First, Kant is not always clear that the fact one wills something entails that one cannot have a duty to do it. It is a duty to preserve one's own life despite the fact "every one also has a direct inclination to do it" (Kant, 2002: 4:397). Second, Sidgwick agrees with Kant that "a psychological law invariably realized in my conduct does not admit of being conceived as 'a precept' or 'dictate' of reason: this latter must be a rule from which I am conscious that it is possible to deviate" (ME 41). Both Sidgwick and Kant agree we frequently fail to *maximize* our own happiness (ME 41–2; 327n1; Kant, 2002: 4:399). Since our own greatest happiness is not, as both allow, what

---

[44] I owe this point and the language to a referee.

we always will, it is not ruled out that we might have a duty to promote our own greatest happiness by the argument Kant wields.

What's more, Kant actually seems at one point to *agree* with Sidgwick on something like E. Kant is alive to the fact that one's present inclination – a "single inclination, well defined as to what it promises and as to the time at which it can be satisfied" (Kant, 2002: 4:399) – can conflict with one's overall happiness ("the satisfaction of all inclinations as a sum"). Lisa might, for instance, wish to feast and drink this evening knowing that this will aggravate her gout and make her on balance worse off in the future. Lisa reasons it is better not to sacrifice the enjoyment of eating for "some possibly groundless expect-ations of happiness allegedly attached to health" (Kant, 2002: 4:399). Kant suggests that there is a clear lack of rationality in this case: "if good health ... did not enter into ... [her] calculations, what would remain, as in other cases [of direct duty], is a law – the law that ... [she] ought to promote ... [her] happiness, not out of inclination, but out of duty. And only from this law would his conduct begin to have real moral worth" (Kant, 2002: 4:399).

Kant's official view is we have only an indirect duty to promote our own happiness. We have this duty only because, empirically, discontent becomes "a *great temptation to transgress one's duties*" (Kant, 2002: 4:399; italics in original; also Kant, 1997b: 5:93) and because "[a]dversity, pain, and want are great temptations to violate one's duty" (Kant, 1996: 6:388). But this is not the best explanation of why Lisa is open to rational criticism. The reason Lisa must avoid the drink and feast is not that doing so will ward off the temptation to vice. We make the judgement that Lisa has reason not to eat and drink well before we have any idea of the impact of doing so on her present or future virtue. The best explanation is that Lisa is irrational. As Sidgwick puts it, "[w]e do not all look with simple indifference on a man who declines to take the right means to attain his own happiness, on no other ground than that he does not care about happiness. Most men would regard such a refusal as irrational" (ME 7). In conflict with his official view, in the *Groundwork* Kant seems to concur with Sidgwick, but his agreement commits him to direct duties to promote one's own (perhaps) greatest happiness.

Kant has another criticism of egoism or self-love; it is a threat to morality (Kant, 1997b: 5:35, 5:93; 1996: 5:378). Kant's point is sometimes that if we make happiness the basis of morality, then there will be no categorical impera-tives (Kant, 2002: 4:441ff.). But his claim is unpersuasive. There is nothing conceptually problematic about categorical imperatives to promote one's own happiness as Sidgwick (following Butler) suggests. Kant's issue seems to be that egoism is a threat to morality because egoism might permit one to lie, commit suicide, masturbate, and stupefy oneself with rich food and fine whisky

(Kant, 1997b: 5:35ff; 1996: 6:421ff.) Kant rejects that these things are permissible.

This is not a rejection of E, for E might be constrained by other moral considerations. Kant seems, then, to reject rational egoism, but he seems to agree with Sidgwick on E. Sidgwick seems, then, to have support for E of the sort set out in the fourth of his tests for higher certainties. But Sidgwick has good reason to be sympathetic to the threat rational egoism poses to morality.

This puts us in a position to investigate at a third criticism of rational egoism. Sidgwick claims at points that utilitarianism's ability to capture, explain and improve the main elements of common-sense morality provides adherents of common-sense morality with rational inducements to believe it (ME 421–2). It seems odd, considering this, that Sidgwick did not take rational egoism's significant conflict with common-sense morality as providing adherents of common-sense morality (among others) with rational inducements to reject it. He insists "flagrant" conflict with common sense is likely to lead to one's method being "declared invalid" (ME 373).[45]

In his main discussion of egoism in Book II of the *Methods*, Sidgwick draws support for rational egoism from common sense and from philosophers.

> it is hardly going too far to say that common sense assumes that 'interested' actions, tending to promote the agent's happiness, are *prima facie* reasonable: and that the *onus probandi* lies with those who maintain that disinterested conduct, as such, is reasonable (ME 120).

> when antagonistic impulses compete for the determination of the Will, we are prompted by the desire for pleasure in general to compare the pleasures which we foresee will respectively attend the gratification of either impulse, and when we have ascertained which set of pleasures is the greatest, Self-love or the desire for pleasure in general reinforces the corresponding impulse. It is thus called into play whenever impulses conflict, and is therefore naturally regulative and directive ... of other springs of action (ME 93–4).

What common sense says does not offer support for rational egoism. At best, it suggests common sense accepts O or E. When Sidgwick describes what common sense believes in respect of egoism he has it saying one has an obligation to one's own greatest happiness (ME 7) or "a duty to seek our own happiness" or to give due concern to our own happiness (ME 327). This is not rational egoism.

He says Clarke, Butler, and Bentham provide some support for egoism (ME 119–20; FC 483–4). But Clarke seems only to say an action cannot be required if it conflicts with the promotion of one's happiness (ME 120; 383n4). Butler's

---

[45] For the claim that egoism is undermined by conflict with common-sense morality, see Schneewind, 1977: 361; Shaver, 1999: 98–108.

view is we have a duty to promote our happiness "within the limits fixed by . . . other [regarding] duties" (ME 327; also 7), or just that we ought to promote our own happiness (ME 386). Bentham agrees only with the claim that "each individual should aim at his own greatest happiness" (ME 119). These philosophers do not seem to support rational egoism.[46] Sidgwick has, instead, support for E of the sort demanded by test 4 of the epistemic tests discussed in Section 2.

Sidgwick does, of course, highlight that rational egoism's support for common-sense prudential beliefs and for some common-sense moral beliefs speaks in its favour (ME 157–8, 162–75). At the same time, Sidgwick acknowledges common sense has an "aversion" to rational egoism (ME 199). He remarks

> A dubious guidance to an ignoble end appears to be all that the calculus of
> Egoistic Hedonism has to offer (ME 200; also 500).

His judgment was harsher in earlier editions, where he says egoism's end is not just ignoble but "despicable" (e.g., ME1 178; ME5 200). The aversion is so strong common sense shrinks from declaring his version of egoism a method of ethics (ME 119; FC 483).[47]

He explains, for example, that while rational egoists will in general favour social order, there may be cases in which they may seek to disrupt peace

> since the disturbance of political order may offer to a cool and skilful person, who
> has the art of fishing in troubled waters, opportunities of gaining wealth, fame,
> and power, far beyond what he could hope for in peaceful times. (ME 165)

And, of course, what is important to the egoist is not actually fulfilling promises or telling the truth but appearing to do so (ME 167–8). This follows because for the egoist it will only be

> generally speaking and for the most part reasonable to conform [to common-
> sense morality] . . . under special circumstances [the rules of common-sense
> morality] must be decisively ignored and broken, – the offence which Egoism
> in the abstract gives to our sympathetic and social nature adds force to the
> recoil from it caused by the perception of its occasional practical conflict with
> common notions of duty. (ME 199)

Egoism has unattractive implications when we consider how it might remedy the defects in some of the main obligations of common-sense morality, including the obligations of veracity and promise-keeping.

---

[46] For a thorough discussion of the extent to which appeal to other philosophers supports rational egoism, see Frankena, 1992; Shaver, 1999: ch. 4.

[47] Sidgwick is not bothered by this. He cares about determining what we have most reason to do. Egoism is a view about this.

My own greatest happiness does not seem to be the relevant consideration to which to appeal in deciding whether to lie to spare an invalid from a dangerous shock or to shield a child from knowledge that it is thought best for her not to have (ME 316). If it is in my self-interest to hasten the death of the invalid to inherit his money, I have an all-things-considered reason to tell him the truth. If I might delight in a child repeating facts which it is better she not know, I seem to have an all-things-considered reason not to lie to the child. These things seem hard to accept. When it comes to deciding whether to realize perfect candour, it does not seem that what maximizes my own greatest happiness is decisive. The impact of what I say on another person seems highly relevant. In the case of promise-keeping, if my neighbour wants the water promised her even though, I hold, the water is potentially harmful to her, the right way to decide what to do does not seem to involve appealing to my own happiness alone. It would be "hard-hearted" to ignore the potential threat to my neighbour's health.

What is perhaps most puzzling of all is that Sidgwick vociferously rejects national egoism while embracing rational egoism. He regards national egoism as anti-moral or immoral (PE 60, 62, 63; EP 299). This is due in part to the fact that, like egoism, it says we ought to conform to the rules of common sense just in case "such conformity will – on the whole and in the long run if not immediately – be conducive to its … interest" (EP 299; also PE 63–4).[48]

In the essay "Public Morality," Sidgwick goes to great lengths to show that the rules binding states are the same as those binding individuals. States ought not to disregard completely the rules of common-sense morality, including the rules of veracity and promise-keeping.

Sidgwick raises several objections to national egoism. One of the objections is that national egoism (unlike rational egoism) fails to gain support from common sense and from philosophers (PE 68). He contends in addition that national egoism is potentially self-defeating. Once it is admitted that nations are exempt from ordinary moral rules, it is likely that "groups and classes" within a nation will feel similarly and act contrary to the "interests of the nation" (PE 69). In short, egoism will beget egoism, to the detriment of national egoism itself.

Sidgwick does not think these arguments are decisive against national egoism. They amount to no more than "bare negation" (PE 70). The popularity of the view, he says, leads him to conclude it comprises

> elements of sound reason in it, which have been exaggerated into dangerous paradox. (PE 70)

---

[48] Sidgwick says that the "immorality" of national egoism begins when "the interest of a particular state is taken as the ultimate and paramount end, justifying the employment of any means whatever to attain it, whatever the consequences of such action may be for the rest of the human race" (PE 64).

Rather perceptively, Sidgwick suggests that the elements of sound reason in the view are clarified once we foreground morality's dependency on a "reasonable expectation of reciprocal observance [of moral rules of justice, veracity, and good faith] on the part of others" (PE 71). If we cannot expect others to behave morally, we make ourselves, if we continue to behave morally, "a prey to others" (PE 71). The effect of having no reasonable expectation of reciprocal observance of moral rules does not, Sidgwick insists, mean that different moral rules apply to states and individuals. Rather, the effect is that, since there is a lot of chicanery and moral transgression in international conduct but not in civilized society, this materially alters "the moral relations between states by extending the rights and duties of self-protection" (PE 74).

In concrete terms, Sidgwick argues that the absence of the expectation of reciprocal observance entails that there are, for states relative to individuals in civilized society, more exceptions to the rules of veracity and fidelity to promises Sidgwick is, however, quick to point out that the strength of such moral rules is relaxed for states only in the presence of (a) urgent need (e.g., to prevent serious espionage or illegitimate occupation of territory) and (b) similar bad acts on the part of the other state with whom the state is dealing (PE 76–7). If other states have lied or failed repeatedly to honour compacts and an urgent need is present, it is permissible for one's own nation to lie or treat compacts less seriously.

But states are not permitted to lie or break promises whenever it is convenient, or aggress without provocation (PE 74). States may even be required to sacrifice on behalf of other states when it is clearly on balance advantageous (PE 80–1). This fits with the common-sense duty

> that we have a general duty of rendering services to our fellow-men and especially to those who are in special need, and that we are bound to make sacrifices for them, when the benefit that we thereby confer very decidedly outweighs the loss to ourselves. (ME 348–9)

Sidgwick implies individuals are at present not in the same condition as the state respecting reciprocity. Individuals have no reason of this sort, then, to depart from ordinary morality. If circumstances changed, individuals would be permitted to diverge from morality along the lines that states might deviate (PE 71).

However, Sidgwick may not fully recognize how even in so-called "civilized" societies individuals often lack reasonable expectation that others will do what they ought. We are constantly in fear or being swindled or cheated or manipulated (think here of phishing scams or cases of so-called "cat fishing") and of not being helped when we need it. In noting this we may see the truth in rational egoism.

One might argue that due to the lack of expectation of reciprocal observance of moral rules, there is a relaxation in some moral rules for individuals at least in some domains as a kind of self-protection. O or E captures the reasonableness of the reluctance to discharge our duties to others or sacrifice on their behalf given that we cannot or might not reasonably expect others to reciprocate. We might argue that this is the truth in rational egoism that explains its favour with thoughtful persons but which "has been exaggerated into a dangerous paradox" (PE 70). We might think concerns about making ourselves "a prey to others" is what lies behind the concern over uncompensated sacrifice. Since we cannot reasonably expect others to sacrifice without compensation (at least when the sacrifice is significant), then we ourselves have good reason not to do it (especially where refraining is the only way to avoid significant harm to our own interests). The important point is that we might be allowed some deviation from common-sense morality on egoistic grounds but only in select, circumscribed situations: where others are not expected to abide by common-sense moral rules and there is an urgent need (to protect our own well-being). And like states we may be required to sacrifice for others in some cases.

In any case, if the reasons given for permitting deviation from common-sense morality in the case of the nation express the truth about when deviation is permissible on egoistic grounds, why does Sidgwick not think they apply to individuals? If he rejects national egoism because it ignores aspects of common-sense morality, why not reject rational egoism for the same reason? If the truth in national egoism does not entail that nations are liberated entirely from common-sense morality, why is the same not true of individuals?

Sidgwick might think in the end there is more to be said in favour of rational egoism than in favour of national egoism. This would perhaps explain the absence of parallel treatment of the two. He says, for example, that, in contrast with national egoism,

> egoism pure and simple, the doctrine that each individual's interest must be
> for him ultimately paramount to all other considerations, there is, in abstract
> ethical discussion, much to be said. (PE 68)

It is not obvious that this is true based on what Sidgwick says. As noted, philosophers and common sense do not seem to support this. On one account of his defence of rational egoism he seems, as we noticed, to rely on an appeal to the distinction between individuals. If it is the case that the distinction between individuals assists in the defence of rational egoism, it might work to note the distinction between nations in defence of national egoism. What is stopping the national egoist from stating that

> The distinction between any one nation and any other is real and fundamental.
> Consequently, we are concerned with the quality of our existence as a nation
> in a sense, fundamentally important, in which we ought not to be concerned

> with the quality of the existence of other nations: and this being so, we do not
> see how it can be proved that this distinction ought not to be taken as
> fundamental in determining the ultimate end of rational action for a nation.[49]

Sidgwick might doubt this works in the case of a nation but, as we have seen, we might doubt it works in the case of an individual. It is very difficult both to reject national egoism and accept rational egoism. Sidgwick did not, it seems, have good reason to cling to rational egoism given its significant conflicts will common-sense morality, conflicts he seems quite sure undermine national egoism and which could be used to undermine rational egoism.

We previously remarked on the fact that Sidgwick admits a theory of morality or rationality may deviate from common sense. However, the limits of such a deviation are, he says, "firmly, though indefinitely, fixed" (ME 373). A method in flagrant conflict with common-sense morality is likely he says, to be declared "invalid."

Sidgwick might have thought affirming a limit that, say, favours utilitarianism over rational egoism would involve arbitrarily excluding the latter. The difficulty is that the national egoist might complain that any limit excluding them but not utilitarianism and egoism would be equally arbitrary.

Sidgwick's attack on national egoism is compelling. It is plausible to think that national egoism is limited by at least some moral considerations. He should have rejected rational egoism for reasons like those he uses to reject national egoism. His case against national egoism is significantly weakened by his unwillingness to properly scrutinize rational egoism. But worse still he misses an opportunity to clarify the truth in egoism and the place of egoistic reasons in moral thinking. He has good reason for thinking that his own inquiries turn up the plausible claim that E (or maybe O) qualifies as a higher certainty. Had he clarified the truth in egoism, it may have been much harder for subsequent philosophers (e.g., Moore, Prichard, and Ross) to blithely ignore the role prudence plays in thinking about what we have most reason to do. Indeed, he might well have made it easier to see how utilitarianism could accommodate the truths in egoism.

Sidgwick ought not to have concluded *The Methods of Ethics* with the dualism of practical reason. At best, he should have concluded that he had support for O and RB and that he was unable to discover a strict priority relation between them.

---

[49] This is, of course, to adapt with the necessary modifications the distinction passage Sidgwick relies on to defend rational egoism (ME 498; FC 484). Hayward, 1901: 146 [italics in original] makes a similar move on behalf of the egoist who rejects temporal neutrality: "We are concerned with the quality of our *present* existence in a sense, fundamentally important, in which we are not concerned with the quality of future existence . . . [t]his concrete principle would stand opposed to the 'prudential' maxim."

Conclusion

Sidgwick's *Methods* is one of the most influential texts in the history of moral philosophy. Sidgwick grapples with some of the most knotty and complex problems in morality. *Sidgwick's Ethics* explored a selection of the intellectual highlights of the *Methods*, including Sidgwick's case in favour of utilitarianism and his argument that rational egoism is no less compelling than utilitarianism and consequently, there exists a dualism at the heart of practical reason. Sidgwick may not have conclusively established the truth of rational egoism or utilitarianism. But there is much value in examining his attempt to defend them and to illustrate their conflict. His discussions provide deep insight into the many factors that matter to defending a moral outlook. Sidgwick relies on an appeal to abstract philosophical intuitions in justifying his moral views. His discussion of how best to avoid error in such intuitions is both distinctive in the history of ethics and informative for contemporary debates. An important part of Sidgwick's defence of both egoism and utilitarianism is his clarification and rejection of the key rules of common-sense morality. Only a very small portion of his clarification and evaluation of the main rules of common-sense morality was discussed here. A full examination of his discussion is worthy of sustained study. Whatever one's view of Sidgwick's arguments happen to be, it cannot be doubted that he presents a vision of how to do moral philosophy that serves to inspire and enrich.

References

Anscombe, G. E. M. (1958). Modern Moral Philosophy. *Philosophy*, **33**(124), 1–19.

Brink, D. (1992). Sidgwick and the Rationale for Rational Egoism. In Bart Schultz, ed., *Essays on Henry Sidgwick*. Cambridge: Cambridge University Press, pp. 199–240.

Brink, D. (1994). Common Sense and First Principles in Sidgwick's Methods. *Social Philosophy and Policy*, **11**(1), 179–201.

Broad, C. D. (1930). *Five Types of Ethical Theory*, London: Routledge & Kegan Paul.

Crisp, R. (2002). Sidgwick and the Boundaries of Intuitionism. In Philip Stratton-Lake, ed., *Ethical Intuitionism: Re-evaluations*. Oxford: Oxford University Press, pp. 56–75.

Crisp, R. (2015). *The Cosmos of Duty: Henry Sidgwick's Methods of Ethics*, Oxford: Oxford University Press.

De Lazari-Radek, K. & Singer, P. (2014). *The Point of View of the Universe: Sidgwick & Contemporary Ethics*, Oxford: Oxford University Press.

Donagan, A. (1992). Sidgwick and Whewellian Intuitionism: Some Enigmas. In Bart Schultz, ed., *Essays on Henry Sidgwick*. Cambridge: Cambridge University Press, pp. 123–42.

Frankena, W. (1992). Sidgwick and the History of Ethical Dualism. In Bart Schultz, ed., *Essays on Henry Sidgwick*. Cambridge: Cambridge University Press, pp. 175–98.

Hayward, F. H. (1901). *The Ethical Philosophy of Sidgwick: Nine Essays, Critical and Expository*, London: Swan Sonnenschein.

Hurka, T. (2014a). Sidgwick on Consequentialism and Deontology: A Critique. *Utilitas*, **26**(2), 129–52.

Hurka, T. (2014b). *British Ethical Theorists from Sidgwick to Ewing*, Oxford: Oxford University Press.

Irwin, T. (2009). *The Development of Ethics: A Historical and Critical Study, Volume III: From Kant to Rawls*, Oxford: Oxford University Press.

Kant, I. (1996). *The Metaphysics of Morals*, ed., Mary Gregor, Cambridge: Cambridge University Press.

Kant, I. (1997a). *Lectures on Ethics*, eds., Peter Heath and J. B. Schneewind, Cambridge: Cambridge University Press.

Kant, I. (1997b). *Critique of Practical Reason*, ed., Mary Gregor, Cambridge: Cambridge University Press.

Kant, I. (2002). *Groundwork for the Metaphysics of Morals*, eds., Thomas E. Hill, Jr. and Arnulf Zweig, Oxford: Oxford University Press.

Miller, D. (2020). The Political Philosophy of Henry Sidgwick. *Utilitas*, **32**(3), 261–75.

Moore, G. E. (1903). *Principia Ethica*, Cambridge: Cambridge University Press.

Nakano-Okuno, M. (2011). *Sidgwick and Contemporary Utilitarianism*, New York: Palgrave Macmillan.

Parfit, D. (1984). *Reasons and Person*, Oxford: Oxford University Press.

Parfit, D. (2011). *On What Matters*, Volume one, Oxford: Oxford University Press.

Phillips, D. (2011). *Sidgwickian Ethics*, Oxford: Oxford University Press.

Rashdall, H. (1924). *The Theory of Good and Evil: A Treatise on Moral Philosophy*, Volume one, 2nd edn., Oxford: Oxford University Press.

Rawls, J. (1974). The Independence of Moral Theory. *Proceedings and Addresses of the American Philosophical Association*, **48**, 5–22.

Ross, W. D. (1930). *The Right and the Good*, Oxford: Oxford University Press.

Ross, W. D. (1939). *Foundations of Ethics*, Oxford: Oxford University Press.

Schneewind, J. B. (1977). *Sidgwick's Ethics and Victorian Moral Philosophy*, Oxford: Oxford University Press.

Schultz, B. (2004). *Henry Sidgwick: Eye of the Universe*, Cambridge: Cambridge University Press.

Schultz, B. (2005). Sidgwick's Racism. In Bart Schultz and Georgios Varouxakis, eds., *Utilitarianism and Empire*. Lanham: Lexington Books, pp. 211–50.

Schultz, B. (2017). *The Happiness Philosophers: The Lives and Works of the Great Utilitarians*, Princeton: Princeton University Press.

Shaver, R. (1999). *Rational Egoism: A Selective and Critical History*, Cambridge: Cambridge University Press.

Shaver, R. (2014). Sidgwick's Axioms and Consequentialism. *Philosophical Review*, **123**(2), 173–204.

Shaver, R. (2020). Sidgwick's Distinction Passage. *Utilitas*, **32**(4), 444–53.

Sidgwick, H. (1870). *The Ethics of Conformity and Subscription*, London: Williams and Norgate.

Sidgwick, H. (1874). ME1. *The Methods of Ethics*, London: Macmillan.

Sidgwick, H. (1876). PC. Professor Calderwood on Intuitionism in Morals. *Mind*, **1**(4), 563–66.

Sidgwick, H. (1877). UG. Hedonism and Ultimate Good. *Mind*, **2**(5), 27–38.

Sidgwick. H. (1877). SE. Mr. Barratt on "The Suppression of Egoism." *Mind*, **2**(7), 411–12.

Sidgwick, H. (1879). FP. The Establishment of Ethical First Principles. *Mind*, **4**(13), 106–11.

Sidgwick, H. (1882). CNSE. Critical Notice of Leslie Stephen, *The Science of Ethics*, *Mind*, **28**(7), 572–86.

Sidgwick, H. (1884). ME3. *The Methods of Ethics*, 3rd edn., London: Macmillan.

Sidgwick, H. (1886). ES. Economic Socialism. *Contemporary Review*, **50**, 620–31.

Sidgwick, H. (1887). IE. Idiopsychological Ethics. *Mind*, **12**(45), 31–44.

Sidgwick, H. (1889). FC. Some Fundamental Ethical Controversies. *Mind*, **14**(56), 473–87.

Sidgwick, H. (1890). ME4. *The Methods of Ethics*, 4th edn., London: Macmillan.

Sidgwick, H. (1891–2). IO. Is the Distinction between "Is" and "Ought" Ultimate and Irreducible? *Proceedings of the Aristotelian Society*, **2**(1), 88–92.

Sidgwick, H. (1893). ME5. *The Methods of Ethics*, 5th edn., London: Macmillan.

Sidgwick, H. (1898). PE. *Practical Ethics: A Collection of Addresses and Essays*, London: Swan Sonnenschein.

Sidgwick, H. (1902). OHE. *Outlines of the History of Ethics for English Readers*, 5th edn., London: Macmillan.

Sidgwick, H. (1902). GSM. *Lectures on the Ethics of T. H. Green, Mr. Herbert Spencer, and J. Martineau*, ed., E. E. Constance Jones, London: Macmillan.

Sidgwick, H. (1902). PSR. *Philosophy, Its Scope and Relations: An Introductory Course of Lectures*, ed., James Ward, London: Macmillan.

Sidgwick, H. (1905). LK. *Lectures on the Philosophy of Kant and Other Philosophical Lectures and Essays*, ed., James Ward, London: Macmillan.

Sidgwick, H. (1981 [1907]). ME. *The Methods of Ethics*, 7th edn., Indianapolis: Hackett.

Sidgwick, H. (1908). EP. *The Elements of Politics*, 3rd edn., London: Macmillan.

Sidgwick, A. & Sidgwick, E. M. (1906). *Henry Sidgwick: A Memoir*, London: Macmillan.

Singer, P. (1974). Sidgwick and Reflective Equilibrium. *The Monist*, **58**(3), 490–517.

Singer, P. (2011). *Practical Ethics*, 3rd edn., Cambridge: Cambridge University Press.

Skelton, A. (2008). Sidgwick's Philosophical Intuitions. *Etica & Politica / Ethics & Politics*, **10**(2), 185–209.

Skelton, A. (2010). Henry Sidgwick's Moral Epistemology. *Journal of the History of Philosophy*, **48**(4), 491–519.

Skelton, A. (2019). Late Utilitarian Moral Theory and Its Development: Sidgwick, Moore. In John Shand, ed., *A Companion to Nineteenth-Century Philosophy*. Oxford: Wiley-Blackwell, pp. 281–310.

Skelton, A. (2022). William David Ross. In Edward N. Zalta, ed., *The Stanford Encyclopedia of Philosophy*, https://plato.stanford.edu/ENTRIES/william-david-ross/.

Smart, J. J. C. (1956). Extreme and Restricted Utilitarianism. *Philosophical Quarterly*, **6**(25), 344–54.

Sullivan, M. (2018). *Time Biases: A Theory of Rational Planning and Personal Persistence*, Oxford: Oxford University Press.

Sverdlik, S. (1985). Sidgwick's Methodology. *Journal of the History of Philosophy*, **23**(4), 537–53.

Williams, B. (1995). The Point of View of the Universe: Sidgwick and the Ambitions of Ethics. In Bernard Williams, ed., *Making Sense of Humanity and Other Philosophical Papers*. Cambridge: Cambridge University Press, pp. 153–71.

Acknowledgements

I wish to thank Roger Crisp and Robert Shaver, who kindly served as referees for Cambridge University Press, Robert Audi, Ben Eggleston, Lisa Forsberg, Dale Miller, Jane Parnell, and the students in the seminar I taught on Sidgwick's Ethics in the autumn of 2020, for helpful feedback on earlier drafts of this Element. I wish also to thank Terry Irwin, Tyler Paytas, and David Phillips for extremely valuable conversations about Sidgwick's ethics and related topics. I gratefully acknowledge the support of the Graham and Gail Wright Distinguished Scholar Award programme and a Social Sciences and Humanities Research Council of Canada Explore Grant (award R3986A06).

Ethics

Ben Eggleston
University of Kansas

Ben Eggleston is a professor of philosophy at the University of Kansas. He is the editor of John Stuart Mill, *Utilitarianism: With Related Remarks from Mill's Other Writings* (Hackett, 2017) and a co-editor of *Moral Theory and Climate Change: Ethical Perspectives on a Warming Planet* (Routledge, 2020), *The Cambridge Companion to Utilitarianism* (Cambridge, 2014), and *John Stuart Mill and the Art of Life* (Oxford, 2011). He is also the author of numerous articles and book chapters on various topics in ethics.

Dale E. Miller
Old Dominion University, Virginia

Dale E. Miller is a professor of philosophy at Old Dominion University. He is the author of *John Stuart Mill: Moral, Social and Political Thought* (Polity, 2010) and a co-editor of *Moral Theory and Climate Change: Ethical Perspectives on a Warming Planet* (Routledge, 2020), *A Companion to Mill* (Blackwell, 2017), *The Cambridge Companion to Utilitarianism* (Cambridge, 2014), *John Stuart Mill and the Art of Life* (Oxford, 2011), and *Morality, Rules, and Consequences: A Critical Reader* (Edinburgh, 2000). He is also the editor-in-chief of *Utilitas*, and the author of numerous articles and book chapters on various topics in ethics broadly construed.

About the Series

This Elements series provides an extensive overview of major figures, theories, and concepts in the field of ethics. Each entry in the series acquaints students with the main aspects of its topic while articulating the author's distinctive viewpoint in a manner that will interest researchers.

For EU product safety concerns, contact us at Calle de José Abascal, 56–1°, 28003 Madrid, Spain or eugpsr@cambridge.org.